# THE MYSTERY OF THE HOLY SPIRIT

# THE MYSTERY OF THE HOLY SPIRIT

BY

## A.W. TOZER

**Bridge-Logos**
Newberry, FL 32669 USA

**Bridge-Logos**

Newberry, FL 32669 USA

Tozer: Mystery of the Holy Spirit
by A.W. Tozer
Edited by Rev. James L. Snyder

Library of Congress Catalog Card Number: 2007920719
International Standard Book Number: 978-0-88270-342-8
International Standard Book Number Hardcover: 978-1-61036-226-9
International Standard Book Number Large Print: 978-1-61036-238-2

Scripture quotations are from the *King James Version* of the Bible.

# Table of Contents

# *Introduction*

THROUGHOUT HIS REMARKABLE MINISTRY, Dr. A. W. Tozer (1897-1963) was recognized as the voice of God while others were mere echoes. His was a clarion call for the church to return to those truths central to her identity in Christ. Thirty-one years of his ministry were spent in Chicago, that "Mecca of Fundamentalists," as Tozer often refers to it. His was often a lone voice when others were following the latest evangelical trend or fad. What he would think of evangelicals today is anyone's guess. I think he would not be too impressed with the level of spirituality found across our country. Many of the things he warned about a generation ago have happened. Some of his warnings are found in this sermon collection. At times, it is hard to remember that Tozer preached these sermons over fifty years ago. The freshness of his themes is indicative of his ministry. He never wasted the congregation's time rehashing the news or the latest fad. His ministry was straight to the heart.

Once he was invited to minister to a group of Brethren in Christ. These people were conservative in their dress and manners, and Tozer was concerned he would not fit in. The Bishop allayed his fears by saying, "Just preach to their hearts, and they will love you." He did, and they did.

This represents the core of his ministry. He always ministered to the heart. And not just any heart, but that heart athirst for God, even the Living God. The curious found him dry and moved on to some titillating preacher, of which there are always plenty. If you had a heart for God and a passion for His presence, you loved Tozer. If, however, you were only interested in advancing some personal agenda, you would find Tozer to be exasperating.

## MYSTERY AND MAJESTY

The theme of this book is a favorite of Tozer: the Holy Spirit. I use the words Mystery and Majesty because these two words put into perspective the teaching on the Holy Spirit found in these sermons. Dr. Tozer probes the mysterious work of the Holy Spirit that no man can fully know. We can experience and understand certain aspects of the Holy Spirit in our life, but for the most part, it is a mystery and wonder, especially to the worshipping heart. Here is the difference. The worshipping heart never looked for answers for the head, but rather sought those assurances of the heart that represent the inexplicable work of the Holy Spirit in the heart of the believer.

Tozer is at his best poking fun at those "preachers" who know more about the Holy Spirit than the Bible discloses. I'm sure he would have pretty much of a hey-day with some of the sheer nonsense passing for biblical teaching on the Holy Spirit. "You can discover," Tozer once instructed, "more of the Holy Spirit in five minutes on your knees in adoring worship than five years at a seminary."

Also, there is a majestic nature to the work of the Holy Spirit in the individual's heart. It is a word that is comparable to nothing. Nothing else or no one else can duplicate the work that the Holy Spirit has to do. Herein lies the problem with contemporary Christians. They have a vague idea of what the Holy Spirit is supposed to do, and because they do not see it happening in their life or in their church, they adopt methods of the world to try to induce a work that only the Holy Spirit can do. Something Tozer considered anathema.

It is interesting to note that the same theological battles prominent in Tozer's day are still in ours. What Tozer has to say in this book is as fresh and appropriate for us today as it was when he first preached the sermons. Keep in mind that these were sermons preached from a pulpit in the church he served in Toronto, Canada. They lack the polish of Tozer's essays. But they do not lack the incisiveness, wit and power associated with Tozer's work and ministry. For lack of a better description, I can say this is raw Tozer. In his sermons he often wandered a bit, but never too far to come back to his main point. Although a quiet man in many regards, Tozer was a lion in the pulpit. He ruled as a king from his pulpit and ministered with the power and authority of the Holy Spirit. His very life and ministry is an illustration and example of the theme of this book.

In Tozer's day, there were two fractions well defined in the area of the doctrine of the Holy Spirit. There were those who did not believe any of the gifts of the Holy Spirit were relevant for today, and therefore should not be sought. They did not believe that a person, after conversion, could be or should be filled with the Holy Spirit. Then there were those on the other side who blew certain aspects of the Spirit, especially tongues, way out of proportion, and failed to see the essential purpose and nature of the Holy Spirit in the life of the believer.

In one of the sermons contained in this volume, Tozer says, "I'm not a traditionalist." He goes on to explain that what he teaches is not because he has believed it. Everything is based upon the Word of God. Everything he believes and teaches must have chapter and verse or it has no validity.

Rev. James L. Snyder

BIOGRAPHY OF

# A.W. TOZER

Adapted from the writings of the
Rev. James L. Snyder, author of
*In Pursuit of God: The Life of A. W. Tozer*

"I fear that we shall never see another Tozer. Men like him are not college bred but Spirit taught."

*Leonard Ravenhill*

# The Early Years:
## His Conversion to Jesus Christ

AIDEN WILSON TOZER was born on April 21, 1897, in La Jose (now Newburg), a tiny farming community in a mountainous region of western Pennsylvania. From early on he preferred using his initials "A. W." rather than his given names.

Tozer was converted to Christ in 1915, when he was seventeen years old. As he was walking home from his work at a rubber factory in Akron, Ohio, he noticed a small gathering of people along the way. There was an old man who was talking to them. Young Aiden went over to investigate the situation because he wondered what the man was talking about.

The speaker had a strong German accent, but it did not take Tozer long to realize that he was preaching to the crowd. Tozer began to wonder about him: "Doesn't this man have a church to preach in? It isn't even Sunday! Why is this old man so excited?"

Aiden was startled out of his thoughts by these words from the preacher: "If you don't know how to be saved, just call on God, saying, 'God, be merciful to me—a sinner,' and God will hear you." Those words burned their way into Tozer's heart, and he could not get the preacher's voice out of his mind. As he walked home, he gave serious thought to what the preacher had said. He had never heard such a message before. The man's words deeply troubled him.

"Saved," he muttered to himself, "'if you don't know how to be saved.' That's what the preacher said." At home, young Tozer headed straight to the attic to be alone so he could think these things through.

A. W. Tozer emerged from that attic as a new creation in Christ Jesus. His was a radical conversion experience, and it was the beginning of a new life, a new world, and a new outlook.

It was Tozer's future mother-in-law who helped him grow in the things of God. She encouraged him to read good books, study the Bible, and pray. She also urged him to preach, and she often gathered people in her home to hear him.

## A MAN OF FAITH AND PRAYER

Though the Tozer home was crowded with Aiden's siblings and several boarders, he managed to find a regular time and place for prayer and Bible study—a small corner of the basement behind the furnace. He cleaned up that spot and set it up as a place to regularly meet with God, his heavenly Father. Here he was able to get alone with God, to pray, meditate, and read the Word of God. This was the foundation for his upcoming ministry.

Aiden's older sister, Essie, would hear her brother groaning in prayer behind the furnace. The first time she heard him, she was frightened; then she realized it was her brother who was praying and "wrestling" with God.

This began a pattern in Tozer's life. He would withdraw from others and seek a quiet place where he could be alone with God. It was then that he also began a habit of taking a small notebook with him in order to keep a journal of his prayers and God's answers to them. Quietness and solitude became very important to him.

## CALLED TO THE MINISTRY
## OF THE GOSPEL OF JESUS CHRIST

He began his Christian ministry five years later. Though he had no formal theological education, his ministry with the Christian and Missionary Alliance would last for forty-four years.

In the early days of his ministry, money was hard to come by. Nonetheless, the Tozers made a pact to trust God for all their needs. He said, "We are convinced that God can send money to His believing children—but it becomes a pretty cheap thing to get excited about the money and fail to give the glory to Him who is the Giver!"

In 1919, Tozer was called to the pastorate of a small, storefront church in Nutter Fort, a little village that was located in the rolling hills of central West Virginia. In these humble beginnings Tozer and his new bride, Ada Cecilia Faust, launched a ministry that continues to influence people to the present day. He later served churches in Indiana and Ohio, as well. The Tozers lived a simple lifestyle with their seven children: six boys and one girl. They never owned a car and always used public transportation.

After serving churches in West Virginia, Ohio, and Indiana, Tozer's next charge proved to be a long-term one. For thirty-one of his forty-four years of ministry he gained prominence as the pastor of Southside Alliance Church in Chicago, Illinois. He served there from 1928 to 1959. He ministered as a pastor, author, editor, Bible conference speaker, and denominational leader. To many people, he was a reliable spiritual mentor.

A commercial illustrator, Francis Chase, attended Tozer's first service in the Chicago church. He said, "He [Tozer] said very little and I didn't expect much. He was slight with plenty of black hair, and certainly not a fashion plate, as we say. He wore a black tie about one and a half inches in width. His shoes were even then outmoded: high tops with hooks part way up. I introduced him and left the platform. He said nothing about being pleased to be there or any other pat phrases usually given on such occasions, but simply introduced his sermon topic, which was, 'God's Westminster Abbey,' based on the eleventh chapter of Hebrews." Francis Chase became a close friend to Tozer through the years.

Tozer's last pastorate was at the Avenue Road Church in Toronto, Canada.

## WRITER AND EDITOR

Tozer always searched for and ministered to those who were hungry for God. He was the editor of *The Alliance Weekly*, the official publication of the Christian and Missionary Alliance. This periodical received a new title in 1958 when it became *The Alliance Witness*, which then became *Alliance Life* in 1987. Under Tozer's leadership, the magazine flourished, and its circulation doubled.

In his first editorial for *The Alliance Weekly* he wrote, "It will cost something to walk slow in the parade of the ages, while excited men of time rush about confusing motion with progress. But it will pay in the long run and the true Christian is not much interested in anything short of that."

*The Alliance Weekly*, more than anything else, helped to establish Tozer as a spokesman to the Evangelical church at large. Many people subscribed to the magazine mainly to read Tozer's prophetic editorials, which were published in Great Britain in *The Life of Faith* magazine. H. F. Stevenson, editor of *The Life of Faith*, said, "His [Tozer's] survey of the contemporary scene was as relevant to Britain as to his own country, so that his articles and books were read avidly here also."

Dr. Nathan Bailey, the late President of the Christian and Missionary Alliance, was likewise amazed at the freshness of Tozer's writings. He said, "In his writings he left the superficial and the obvious and the trivial for others to toss around, giving himself to the discipline of study and prayer that resulted in articles and books that reached deep into the hearts of men."

Tozer wrote many books, as well. Some of his best-known works include: *Let My People Go*; *Man: the Dwelling Place of God*; *Paths to Power*; *The Divine Conquest*; *The Knowledge of the Holy*; *The Pursuit of God*; *The Root of the Righteous*; *The Attributes of God*; *The Radical Cross*; *Whatever Happened to Worship?*; and *Warfare of the Spirit*.

Dr. Tozer's books sprang from a deeply burdened heart. He had a message from God that he knew he had to give. In his preface to *The Divine Conquest* (now entitled *The Pursuit of God*), he explained, "The sight of the languishing church around me and the operation of a new spiritual power within me have set up a pressure impossible to resist. Whether or not the book ever reaches a wide public, still it has to be written if for no other reason than to relieve an unbearable burden on the heart."

The last literary work he created was completed just before his death and was published posthumously several months after he went home to be with his Lord. It was entitled *The Christian Book of Mystical Verse*. This volume was a compilation of a wealth of mystic poetry that had blessed Tozer's heart throughout the years. In the introduction of this book he defined "mystic" as follows: "The word 'mystic' as it occurs in the title of this book refers to that personal spiritual experience common to the saints of Bible times and well known to multitudes of persons in the post-biblical era. I refer to the evangelical mystic who has been brought by the gospel into intimate fellowship with the Godhead. His theology is no less and no more than is taught in the Christian Scriptures. He walks the high road of truth where walked of old prophets and apostles, and where down the centuries walked martyrs, reformers, Puritans, evangelists and missionaries of the cross. He differs from the ordinary orthodox Christian only because he experiences his faith down in the depths of his sentient being while the other does not. He exists in a world of spiritual reality. He is quietly, deeply, and sometimes almost ecstatically aware of the Presence of God in his own nature and in the world around him. His religious experience is something elemental, as old as time and the creation. It is immediate acquaintance with God by union with the Eternal Son. It is to know that which passes knowledge." (From *The Christian Book of Mystical Verse*, Christian Publications, Harrisburg, PA.)


## A DAILY WALK WITH GOD

The preceding paragraph gives an apt description of Tozer's daily walk with God. He had a profound sense of God that enveloped him in reverence and adoration. His one daily exercise was the practice of the presence of God, pursuing Him with all his strength and energy. To him, Jesus Christ was a daily wonder, a recurring astonishment, and a continual amazement of love and grace.

Tozer was a man of prayer. He often commented, "As a man prays, so is he." His entire ministry flowed out of fervent prayer.

His sermons were powerful, and his outstanding books established him as a classic devotional writer. In addition, Tozer had a weekly radio broadcast that was aired on WMBI—the radio station of the Moody Bible Institute in Chicago. His program was called "Talks From a Pastor's Study," and those talks emanated from Tozer's study at Southside Alliance Church. As a result of those broadcasts, he received frequent invitations to minister at Chicago-area Bible colleges, which he greatly enjoyed.

To truly understand Tozer, one must focus on his devotional life. For him, correct doctrine was not enough. He said, "You can be straight as a gun barrel theologically and as empty as one spiritually." When he preached and taught, he did not stress systematic theology; instead, he emphasized the importance of a personal relationship with God—a relationship so personal and so overpowering as to entirely captivate a person's attention. He longed for what he called a "God-conscious soul"—a heart that is aflame for God.

He constantly called evangelicals to return to the authentic biblical positions that had characterized the Church when it was most faithful to Christ and His Word. While his messages were profound and sober, Tozer spiced them with his wonderful sense of humor. However, one will find little of his humor in his books.

Tozer loved to have fellowship with God. He once wrote, "I have found God to be cordial and generous and in every way easy to live with." In a similar vein he wrote, "Labor that does not spring out of worship is futile and can only be wood, hay, and stubble in the day that shall try every man's work."

A. W. Tozer loved hymns, and he acquired an extensive collection of old hymnals. He often used these hymnals as means for meditation and devotional reading. Often, he would counsel people to get a hymnbook—"but don't get one that is less than a hundred years old." In one of his articles for *The Alliance Weekly* he wrote, "After the Bible the next most valuable book for the Christian is a good hymnal. Let any young Christian spend a year prayerfully meditating on the hymns of [Isaac] Watts and [Charles] Wesley alone, and he will become a fine theologian. Then let him read a balanced diet of the Puritans and the Christian mystics. The results will be more wonderful than he could have dreamed."

## THE IMPORTANCE OF WORSHIP

Worship was vitally important to Tozer. He wrote, "Worship is to feel in your heart and express in some appropriate manner a humbling but delightful sense of admiring awe, astonished wonder, and overpowering love in the presence of that most ancient Mystery, that Majesty which philosophers call the First Cause, but which we call Our Father in Heaven."

Tozer's hunger for God led him to study the Christian mystics, and in them he found a deep knowledge of God and absorbing love for Him, which propelled him to go deeper with God. He said, "These people know God, and I want to know what they know about God and how they came to know it."

Mr. Ray McAfee was the associate pastor, choir director, and song leader for Dr. Tozer in Chicago for fifteen years. They often met together for prayer and conversation. McAfee wrote, "On a day that I shall never forget, Tozer knelt down by his chair, took off his glasses and laid them on the chair, rested back on his bent ankles. He clasped his hands together, raised his face with his eyes closed and began, 'O God, we are before Thee.' With that there came a rush of God's presence that literally filled the room, and we both worshiped God in silent ecstasy, wonder, and adoration."

McAfee went on, "I've never forgotten that moment, and I don't want to forget it. The memory lingers in my mind, almost with the same freshness and vivacity as that morning. That, to me, was Dr. Tozer."

### THE BEAT OF A "DIFFERENT DRUMMER"

Tozer, of course, was not a perfect man. He had the disposition of a recluse at times and a very heavy schedule. This left little time for his wife, Ada, and their children. Many, even members of his own family, did not truly understand him, particularly when he insisted on being alone so often. Some people even regarded him as being a bit odd, but what others thought of him did not bother Tozer in the least. His primary business was the worship of God, and nothing else really mattered all that much to him.

Tozer marched to the beat of "a different drummer," but not in the same way a rebel might do. It was simply that he was totally sold out to Jesus Christ. His family, friends, and even the ministry had to take a back seat to his pursuit of God. He entitled one of his essays, "The Saint Must Walk Alone," and this provides us with important insights into his perspective and priorities.

At times he would come to the family dinner table, especially after the children had left, and not speak a word—not because he was mad at anyone, but because he was completely focused on God, and he refused to violate that focus even for fellowship around the table with family and friends. In light of this, Tozer did not spend much time perfecting his "social graces."

Tozer loved to be shut in alone with God. He cultivated his ability to focus on Him every day. In so doing, he would quiet his heart and adore and worship his heavenly Father.

At conferences it often seemed as if Tozer was preoccupied with something, which he was, because he was musing about some aspect of the God he loved so much. He told others that he had dreams of God, as well, so his focus on God continued even after he went to sleep!

Tozer generously shared the lessons he had learned through worship with all who seemed interested. He firmly believed that his ministry had to flow from worship and that any work that does not flow from worship is unacceptable to God.

He never entangled himself in social or political issues, even though he was highly opinionated regarding many of them. As a minister of the gospel, however, he realized that his job was to preach the good news and to lead people to Jesus. Because of this, his writings are as fresh today as they were when he first wrote them; they appeal to the essential needs of human beings, regardless of the age in which they live.

Tozer criticized entertainment in churches, and this made him somewhat infamous and less popular with some Christians. This attitude stemmed from his high regard for worship, which he felt was violated oftentimes by attempts to bring entertainment to God's people. To him, worship was to be pure and untainted by worldly things.

Tozer, like many other preachers, was greatly concerned about the ways in which worldliness was making inroads in the Church and how it was affecting Christians. He was particularly critical of some forms of evangelism, which he felt lowered the standards that the Church should be upholding.

## HIS GOAL IN PREACHING

Tozer's goal in preaching was to lead the listener straight into the presence of God. Therefore, everything that would distract from the message, and particularly from God, he ruthlessly cut out.

In prayer God would lay a burden on Tozer's heart. Then, as time passed, he would preach a series of sermons related to this burden. When he was away from his own pulpit, he would preach the same sermons to others. As he did so, sometimes the weight of the burden would increase. Sometimes it would weigh him down to the point that even in preaching he could find no release. This would then lead him to begin writing and the fruit would eventually take the form of a book.

In 1945, Dr. Tozer was preaching along a particular line of Bible truth. Shortly before this, he had experienced a fresh encounter with God and was sharing this meaningful experience with his congregation. The sermons were richly blessed of God, and the people in the Chicago church were deeply touched by them.

As he went forth to preaching missions in other locations, he continued to share his experience with each congregation. In preaching these sermons he sensed a strange pressure building within himself. At first this phenomenon confused him, but after long hours of prayer and meditation, he began to see how God was leading him.

About this same time, Dr. Tozer received an invitation to preach in McAllen, Texas. He reasoned that this would be an opportunity for him to do something about the burden and the pressure he was experiencing. He was certain that the long train ride from Chicago to Texas would give him ample time for thinking and writing.

He wrote all night, as the Pullman train rumbled through the middle part of America. The subject he was writing about had taken full control of him.

When the train pulled into the station the next morning, the rough draft of the book was finished. It was later published as *The Pursuit of God*, a very successful bestseller. To date, the book has sold over 1,000,000 copies, and it has been translated into a multitude of languages for readers around the world.

Tozer's method of preaching included the strong declaration of biblical principles, never merely an involvement in word studies, clever outlines, or statistics. Listening to his recorded sermons or reading any of his many books, the observer will notice the absence of alliteration. His style was the simple unfolding of truth as naturally as a flower unfolds in the sunlight.

According to Tozer, every preacher must develop the habit of "reading good writing." He urged people to go back to the classics and said, "Read some of the great Puritan authors and some of the mystics. Read and memorize good poetry. Observe how these writers express themselves. Become word conscious. Pay attention to words and the effect they have. Get and use a dictionary. Whenever I come across a word I'm not familiar with, I look it up immediately and study it. With a large vocabulary you are able to be precise in what you are saying. Nothing takes the place of using the right word. Flaubert used to say there are no synonyms. Find the right word, and use it."

One of Tozer's trademarks in preaching was that he always seemed to have the right word at his disposal.

There were many times when Tozer preached and his audiences felt that they were standing on the holy mount, witnessing the Savior transfigured before them and, like Peter, never wanting to leave.

Psalm 104, a meditation upon the majesty and providence of God, thrilled Tozer's heart, and he often preached from it. At the close of one of the sermons he gave on Psalm 104, a member of the congregation stated, "He out-Davided David!"

Clearly, he was a defender of the faith that was once delivered unto the saints. He once made this statement: "I believe everything is wrong until God sets it right."

## TOZER'S LEGACY

The legacy left by Tozer is found in the majesty of God. His supreme desire was to exalt the Lord Jesus Christ. "If you major on knowing God," Tozer once wrote, "and cultivate a sense of His presence in your daily life, and do what Brother Lawrence advises, 'Practice the presence of God' daily and seek to know the Holy Spirit in the Scriptures, you will go a long way in serving your generation for God. No man has any right to die until he has served his generation."

Tozer was recognized by many as being a prophet to the Body of Christ. Because he was such a respected man of God, many would come to him for advice and counsel, including students from nearby Wheaton College. Tozer said, "Years ago I prayed that God would sharpen my mind and enable me to receive everything He wanted to say to me. I then prayed that God would anoint my head with the oil of the prophet so I could say it back to the people. That one prayer has cost me plenty since, I can tell you that. Don't ever pray such a prayer if you don't mean it, and, if you want to be happy, don't pray it, either."

Regarding his preaching, he said, "I like to compare the preacher to an artist. An artist works in water, oil, sand, stone, gold, glass. On the other hand, the preacher works in the stuff called mankind. The artist has an idea of abstract beauty and he seeks to reproduce it in visible, concrete things. The preacher has Christ and tries to make Him visible in human lives. The artist has genius while the preacher has the Holy Spirit. The artist draws his inspiration from other artists while the preacher draws his inspiration in prayer alone with God.

"The tools of the artist are brushes, chisels, paint. But the tools of the preacher are words. Ninety-nine percent of your public service will be using words. A preacher, like the artist, must master his tools. He must toil and labor and strive for mastery in this area. At first he will make awkward attempts, but if he keeps at it, he will become an expert."

Regarding his preparation for preaching, Tozer said, "Many times I come here to my study as uninspired as a burnt shingle. I have editorials due, the preaching ministry here, plus outside preaching engagements. Often when I come here I kneel by that old sofa over there with my Bible and a hymn book. I'll read some Scripture, softly sing a few hymns and in a short time my heart is worshiping God. God begins to manifest Himself to me and pour matter into my soul. Before long I take up my pencil and begin jotting down sketches and outlines for editorials and sermons."

Toward the end of his ministry, Tozer asked for prayer from his congregation. He said, "Pray for me in the light of the pressures of our times. Pray that I will not just come to a wearied end—an exhausted, tired old preacher, interested only in hunting a place to roost. Pray that I will be willing to let my Christian experience and Christian standards cost me something right down to the last gasp!"

On May 12, 1963, A. W. Tozer's earthly labors ended. His faith in God's majesty became sight as he entered His presence. At the funeral his daughter Becky said, "I can't feel sad; I know Dad's happy; he's lived for this all his life."

Although his physical presence has been removed from us, Tozer will continue to minister to those who are thirsty for the things of God. Some have referred to him as the "conscience of evangelicalism." As such, he recognized modern Christianity sailing through a dense spiritual fog and pointed out the rocks on which it could flounder if it continued its course. His spiritual intention enabled him to scent error, name it for what it was and reject it—all in one decisive act.

Tozer was buried in Ellet Cemetery in Akron, Ohio. His epitaph gives us a precise description of him: "A. W. Tozer—a Man of God."

## —☙ TOZER-GRAMS ❧—

"It is doubtful whether God can bless a man greatly until He has hurt him deeply."

"Faith is seeing the invisible, but not the nonexistent."

"Our religious activities should be ordered in such a way as to leave plenty of time for the cultivation of the fruits of solitude and silence."

"I am convinced that the dearth of great saints in this day is due at least in part to our unwillingness to give sufficient time to the cultivation of the knowledge of God."

"God discovers Himself to 'babes' and hides Himself in thick darkness from the wise and the prudent. We must simplify our approach to Him. We must strip down to essentials, and they will be found to be blessedly few."

## Prayer

*Lord, I would trust Thee completely; I would be altogether Thine; I would exalt Thee above all. I desire that I may feel no sense of possessing anything outside of Thee. I want constantly to be aware of Thy overshadowing Presence and to hear Thy speaking Voice. I long to live in restful sincerity of heart. I want to live so fully in the Spirit that all my thought may be as sweet incense ascending to Thee and every part of my life may be an act of worship. Therefore I pray in the word of Thy great servant of old, "I beseech Thee so for to cleanse the intent of mine heart with the unspeakable gift of Thy grace, that I may perfectly love Thee and worthily praise Thee." And all this I confidently believe Thou wilt grant me through the merits of Jesus Christ Thy Son. Amen."*

# *Photo Gallery*

AIDEN WILSON TOZER
1897 – 1963

Very few photographs were taken of A.W. Tozer.
This one was taken in 1956.

Tozer in 1959.

A simple inscription marks Tozer's grave near Akron, Ohio.

# The Mystery
## of the
## Holy Sprit

BY A.W. TOZER

CHAPTER 1

# Who Is the Holy Spirit?

YOU WILL NOTICE I use interchangeably the words "Spirit" and "Ghost." They mean exactly and precisely the same thing. Our English word "Ghost " comes from the old Anglo-Saxon word "gast" and means "Spirit." The phrase "Holy Ghost" comes from the old Elizabethan and pre-Elizabethan English the "holy gast." Therefore, it makes no difference, which I say, I mean the same thing.

Let me start by reminding you that about a century ago the theological liberals in our country committed a great blunder. That blunder took the form of neglecting or denying the deity of Jesus. They either did not talk about it at all, or else they explained the deity of Jesus away, and neglected to mention His lordship over the Church. This was a stupid and dangerous blunder, which brought inner blindness to thousands and spiritual decay and death to greater thousands.

The evangelical church made up of gospel Christians such as you and me, people who believe the Bible, have committed a comparable blunder. That blunder took the form of neglecting or denying the deity of the Holy Spirit.

I need to modify that, for I doubt whether any Evangelical ever denied the deity of the Holy Spirit. However, we certainly neglect Him and His lordship within the Church. This failure to honor the Holy Spirit has resulted in much desolation within the Church.

For one, the fellowship of the Church has degenerated into a social fellowship with a mild religious flavor. For me, either I want God or I do not want anything at all to do with religion. I could never get interested in some old maids social club, with a little bit of Christianity thrown in to give it respectability. Either I want it all or I do not want any. I want God or I am perfectly happy to go out and be something else. I think the Lord had something like that in mind when He said, "I know thy works, that thou art neither cold nor hot: I would thou wert cold or hot," (Revelation 3:15 KJV).

Another result of the failure to honor the Holy Ghost is that so many non-spiritual, un-spiritual and anti-spiritual features have been brought into the church. The average church could not run on a hymnbook and a Bible. The church started out with a Bible and then developed a hymnbook, and for years, that was enough. Now, some people could not serve God without at least one vanload of equipment to keep them happy. All this attraction to win people and keep them coming may be fine, it may be elevated, it may be cheap, it may be degrading, it may be coarse, it may be artistic; but it all depends on who is running the show. Because the Holy Spirit is not the center of attraction, and the Lord is not the one in charge, we must bring in all sorts of anti-scriptural and un-scriptural claptrap to keep the people happy and keep them coming.

The horrible part is not so much that this is true, but that it needs to be at all. The great woe is not the presence of religious toys and trifles, but the necessity for them because the presence of the Eternal Spirit is not in our midst. The tragedy and woe of the hour is trying to make up for His absence by doing these things to keep our own spirits up.

I mentioned once in a sermon in Chicago that some churches are so completely out of the hands of God, if the Holy Ghost withdrew from them, they would not find it out for three months. Afterward I received a telephone call from a woman.

The voice on the phone said, "Mr. Tozer, I am not a member of your church; I am a member of a church on the north side."

If you know anything about that great city, you know that being on the north side is like being in another state.

She said, "I was down to your church last night and heard you say that there are churches where, if the Holy Spirit should desert them, they'd never find it out. Mr. Tozer, I want you to know that's what has happened in our church."

Her voice was tender and broken, there was no criticism, and I tried to console her.

"Well, maybe," I said, "it's just that He is grieved, or maybe He's not given His place."

"No," she said, "it's past that, Mr. Tozer. We have so consistently rejected Him in our church that He is gone; He is no longer here."

Now, I doubt whether she is right. I do not believe the Spirit of God ever leaves the church completely, but He can, like the Savior who was asleep in the hinder part of the ship, go to sleep and not make Himself known and let us get along without Him for years.

To fully understand this I must ask you to shake your head real hard and wake up some of those cells that have not had a good workout since you got out of college. I'm going to ask you to think with me about something that is a little bit off the beaten track.

Let me pose a simple question. What is the Holy Spirit?

In the first place, spirit is another mode of being than matter. You can pick a thing up and bounce it around; that is matter. You and I are composed of matter. That head you have is matter. That is only one mode of existence, but there is another, and that is spirit.

The difference between matter and spirit is that matter possesses weight, size, color and extension in space. It can be measured and weighed and has form. But the Holy Spirit is not material, therefore He does not have weight or dimension or shape or extension in space.

One power of spirit is to penetrate matter and things and all substances. Your spirit, for instance, dwells in your body somewhere, and it penetrates your body without hurting the body. It is in there penetrating because it is another form.

When Jesus had risen from the dead and was no more mere matter, He came into a locked room through the wall somehow, and managed to penetrate and get into that room without unlocking the door. He could not have done that prior to his death, but He did it afterward. Spirit, then, is another kind of substance. It is different from material things and can penetrate personality. Your spirit can penetrate your personality. One personality can penetrate another personality. The Holy Spirit can penetrate your personality and your spirit. The Bible refers to this in 1 Corinthians, "For what man knoweth the things of a man, save the spirit of man which is in him? Even so the things of God knoweth no man, but the Spirit of God," (1 Corinthians 2:11 KJV). Therefore, the Spirit of God can penetrate the spirit of man.

Let me mention what the Holy Spirit is not.

The Holy Spirit is not enthusiasm. Some people get enthusiasm and imagine it is the Holy Spirit. They become worked up over a song thinking it is Spirit-anointed worship. And they imagine that is the Spirit. Enthusiasm is not the Holy Spirit, because those same people go out and live just like the world. The Holy Spirit never enters a man and then lets him live like the world. You can be sure of that.

Incidentally, that is the reason most people do not want to be filled with the Holy Spirit; they want to live the way they want to live and have the Holy Spirit as a bit of something extra, as you might have a diamond stickpin or something very beautiful on your clothing. They want the Holy Ghost to be something added, but the Holy Spirit will not be an addition. The Holy Spirit must be Lord or He will not come at all.

The Holy Spirit is not courage, or energy, or the personification of all good qualities, like Jack Frost is the personification of cold weather and Santa Claus the personification of wanting to give someone a tie. The Holy Spirit is not a personification of anything, but the Holy Spirit is a person just the same as you are a person. He has all the qualities of a person. The Holy Spirit has substance but not material substance. He has individuality. He is one being and not another. He has will and He has intelligence and He has feeling and He has knowledge, sympathy, and the ability to love and see and think and hear and speak and desire and grieve and rejoice. And Jesus said about the Holy Spirit, "But when the Comforter is come, whom I will send unto you from the Father, even the Spirit of truth, which proceedeth from the Father, He shall testify of Me" (John 15:26 KJV).

I have said the Holy Spirit is spirit and not matter. He is personality, He is individuality. He has intelligence, love, memory and can communicate with you. He can love you and therefore can be grieved when you grieve Him. He can be quenched, as any friend can be if you turn on Him, of course He will be hushed into hurt silence, because you have wounded Him. Therefore, we can wound the Holy Spirit.

Now, that is what He is. But, who is the Holy Spirit?

Consider the testimony of the Church down through the years. The historic church has consistently given witness that the Holy Spirit is God. Those who attended some of the denominational churches are familiar with the Nicene Creed, quoted every so often.

There is another creed called the Athanasian Creed. That came into being when a man stood up and said that Jesus was a good man and a great man, but He was not God. He was not divine, nor was He the second person of the Trinity. In response to this heresy, another man responded by declaring the Bible teaches that Jesus is God. All kinds of controversy erupted around this doctrine.

Finally, some came to Athanasia and said, "Athanasia, the whole world is against you on this." He said, "All right, then I'm against the whole world." He did not mind having them against him, he stood his ground.

This came to a peak at a great gathering at Nice, and out of it came the Athanasian Creed. The Church Fathers got together, and they hammered out what the Bible had to say about the Three Persons of the Trinity. Most of us are so busy reading religious fiction that we never get around to it. Therefore, I thought it might be beneficial if I took you back about 1,300 years and listened to our Fathers tell about who God is.

## THE ATHANASIAN CREED

Whosoever will be saved, before all things it is necessary that he hold the catholic [i.e., universal, Christian] faith. Which faith except every one do keep whole and undefiled, without doubt he shall perish everlastingly. And the catholic faith is this, that we worship one God in Trinity, and Trinity in Unity; Neither confounding the Persons, nor dividing the Substance. For there is one Person of the Father, another of the Son, and another of the Holy Ghost. But the Godhead of the Father, of the Son, and of the Holy Ghost is all one: the glory equal, the majesty coeternal. Such as the Father is, such is the Son, and such is the Holy Ghost. The Father uncreated, the Son uncreated, and the Holy Ghost uncreated. The Father incomprehensible, the Son incomprehensible, and the Holy Ghost incomprehensible. The Father eternal, the Son eternal, and the Holy Ghost eternal. And yet they are not three Eternals, but one Eternal. As there are not three Uncreated nor three Incomprehensibles, but one Uncreated and one Incomprehensible. So likewise the Father is almighty, the Son almighty, and the Holy Ghost almighty. And yet they are not three Almighties, but one Almighty. So the Father is God, the Son is God, and the Holy Ghost is God. And yet they are not three Gods, but one God. So likewise the Father is Lord, the Son Lord, and the Holy Ghost Lord. And yet not three Lords, but one Lord. For like as we are compelled by the Christian verity to acknowledge every Person by Himself to be God and Lord, So are we forbidden by the catholic religion to say, There be three Gods, or three Lords.

The Father is made of none: neither created nor begotten. The Son is of the Father alone; not made, nor created, but begotten. The Holy Ghost is of the Father and of the Son: neither made, nor created, nor begotten, but proceeding. So there is one Father, not three Fathers; one Son, not three Sons; one Holy Ghost, not three Holy Ghosts. And in this Trinity none is before or after another; none is greater or less than another; But the whole Three Persons are coeternal together, and coequal: so that in all things, as is aforesaid, the Unity in Trinity and the Trinity in Unity is to be worshiped. He, therefore, that will be saved must thus think of the Trinity.

Furthermore, it is necessary to everlasting salvation that he also believes faithfully the incarnation of our Lord Jesus Christ. For the right faith is that we believe and confess that our Lord Jesus Christ, the Son of God, is God and Man; God of the Substance of the Father, begotten before the worlds; and Man of the substance of His mother, born in the world; Perfect God and perfect Man, of a reasonable soul and human flesh subsisting. Equal to the Father as touching His Godhead, and inferior to the Father as touching His manhood; Who, although He be God and Man, yet He is not two, but one Christ: One, not by conversion of the Godhead into flesh, but by taking the manhood into God; One altogether; not by confusion of Substance, but by unity of Person. For as the reasonable soul and flesh is one man, so God and Man is one Christ; Who suffered for our salvation; descended into hell, rose again the third day from the dead; He ascended into heaven; He sitteth on the right hand of the Father, God Almighty; from whence He shall come to judge the quick and the dead. At Whose coming all men shall rise again with their bodies, and shall give an account of their own works. And they that have done good shall go into life everlasting; and they that have done evil, into everlasting fire.

This is the catholic faith; which except a man believe faithfully and firmly, he cannot be saved.

I do not know what something like that does to you, but that is just like a chicken dinner to my soul, to know this has come down the years and is what our Fathers believed. When that company of Christians met and declared this kind of thing, some had their tongues pulled out, some had their ears burned off, some had their arms torn off and some lost a leg all because they stood for this thing; that Jesus is Lord to the glory of God the Father. The Romans persecuted them under Diocletian, Caligula, and the rest of them. These men were martyrs who hadn't quite died, but who were maimed horribly. Old saints of God and scholars, who knew the truth, came together, wrote this and gave it to the world and for the ages. And I thank God on my knees for them.

Not only does the historic church say that the Holy Spirit is God, but the Scriptures say that the Holy Spirit is God.

If the Church said it and the Scripture did not say it, I would reject it. I would not believe an Archangel if he came to me with a wingspread of twelve feet shining like an atom bomb just at the moment it goes off, if he could not give me chapter and verse. I want to know it is here in the book.

I am not a traditionalist. Anybody comes to me and says this is traditional; I will say, "all right, interesting, if true but, is it true? Give me chapter and verse." All tradition must bow in reverence before the clear testimony of God's Word.

What I want to know is, were these old brethren, when they said all this, were they telling the truth? Well, listen to what the scriptures have to say.

The Scripture says He's God, gives to Him the attributes that belong to God and the Son and the Father. For instance, the 139th Psalm says, "Whither shall I go from thy spirit? or whither shall I flee from thy presence?" (Psalms 139:7). That is omnipresence. Not even the devil is omnipresent. Only God can claim omnipresence. The Psalmist attributed omnipresence to the Holy Spirit.

Then in Job, He is given the power to create. "By his spirit he hath garnished the heavens; his hand hath formed the crooked serpent." (Job 26:13).

And he said, "The spirit of God hath made me, and the breath of the Almighty hath given me life," (Job 33:4). There we have the breath, the "gast," the "ghost," the Spirit of the Almighty has given me life. Therefore, the Holy Spirit here is said to be Creator. He issues commands, "Thus saith the Spirit," and only God can do that.

Then there is the baptismal formula. "I baptize you in the name of the Father, and of the Son, and of the Holy Ghost."

There is the benediction, "The grace of Christ, and the love of God, and the communion of the Holy Ghost."

This may be a little shocking, but I want to ask you; if the Spirit of God was not God, but something less, if He was a man or an angel, or something else; if He just was not God as some people say, how would it sound if I introduced the name of someone else? The archangel, Gabriel, for instance.

Suppose I said, "I baptize you in the name of the Father and the Son and Saint Paul." Wouldn't that be a shocking, horrible thing? If I said, "I baptize you in the name of the Father and the Son and the Virgin Mary." Wouldn't that be a horrible thing? For you cannot attribute deity to Saint Paul. You cannot attribute deity to the Virgin, although we honor her, because she was the mother of our Lord. The Mother of our Lord's body, but not the mother of the Lord's deity. For His deity had been before the foundation of the world. "In the beginning was the Word, and the Word was with God, and the Word was God ... and all things were made by him; and without him was not anything made that was made." And the holy Lord, whom she bore, had made the very atoms that composed the body of His mother. Suppose we introduced her there, or introduced Gabriel the Archangel there? And we would say "the grace of our Lord Jesus Christ, the love of God and the communion of the Archangel Gabriel."

Everyone would run for the door. They would say, "There's heresy in that church." It would be a horrible thing to introduce an archangel or a man in where the Holy Spirit belongs, never, never, my brother. The Holy Spirit is God, and the most important thing here tonight is that the Holy Spirit is present. There is unseen deity present.

I cannot bring Him here. I can only tell you that He is here. That is all. I can tell you that He is present in our midst, a knowing, feeling personality. He knows how you are reacting to what I am saying. He knows why you came. He knows what you are going to say as soon as you get out on the sidewalk. He knows how you are thinking now. He knows your "uprising and your down sitting" and understands your thoughts afar off. And you cannot hide from Him. He is present in our midst. "I will send another Comforter, to you and He will abide with you." Therefore, He is here among us. We meet as Christians, and there is an invisible presence among our assembly. We cannot see Him but we know He is present.

He is indivisible from the Father and the Son. In addition, He is all God and exercises all the rights of God, and He merits all worship, all love and all obedience.

That is who the Holy Spirit is. And here is a beautiful thing about the Holy Spirit: being the Spirit of Jesus you will find Him exactly like Jesus. Many people have been frightened by people claiming to be filled with the Spirit and acting anyway else but like the Spirit. Some people say when they are filled with the Spirit they are very stern, harsh and abusive. Others do weird things and say that is the Holy Spirit. The Holy Spirit is exactly like Jesus, just as Jesus is exactly like the Father. "He that hath seen me hath seen the Father," said Jesus. "I will send you another Comforter, and he will take the things of mine and show them unto you." In other words Jesus is saying, "He will demonstrate me to you."

What does the Holy Spirit think of babies? Well, what did Jesus think of babies? He thought of babies just what the Father did. And the Father must think wonderfully well of babies because the Son took a baby in His arms, put His hand on his little baldhead and said, "God bless you."

Maybe theologians do not know why He did it, but I think I do. Nothing is sweeter and softer in the entire world than the top of a little baby's head. Jesus put His hand on that little soft head and blessed it in the name of His Father. The Holy Spirit is the Spirit of Jesus. What does the Spirit think of babies, then? The Spirit thinks of babies exactly what Jesus did.

What does the Spirit think of sick people? Well, what did Jesus think of sick people?

What does the Spirit think of sinful people? What did Jesus think of the woman, dragged into His presence, taken in adultery? The Spirit feels exactly the way Jesus feels about everything. He is the Spirit of Jesus and He acts exactly the way Jesus acts. If Christ Jesus our Lord was to walk down our church aisle and we could think Him here, no person would run from Him. Nobody. Mothers brought their babies, the sick came, the weary came, the tired came, the dispossessed came. Everybody came, because He was the most magnetic person that ever lived. Even old Fredrick Nietzsche, that nihilistic German philosopher that brought on world wars I and II, and laid the foundation for the Nazis. That old, ungodly fellow said, "I love Jesus, but I hate that man Paul." He could not take Paul but he loved Jesus.

You will not find anybody saying very much against Jesus personally, because Jesus was the most winsome, the most loving, the most kindly, the tenderest, the most beautiful character that ever lived in the entire world. And you know what He was? He was demonstrating the Spirit. That is the way the Spirit is.

The Holy Spirit is friendly. We try to make Him something else but friendly, but He is friendly. Because He is friendly, He can be grieved. We can grieve Him by ignoring Him, by resisting Him, by doubting Him or by sinning against Him. We grieve Him by refusing to obey Him, by turning our backs on Him.

Keep in mind, there must be love present before there can be grief. Let me give you an example.

Suppose you had a seventeen-year-old son who began to go bad, who got to that age where he wanted to take things into his own hand. Suppose he joined up with some boy you did not know, some stranger from another part of town, and they got into trouble. You were called down to the police station and there sat your boy, and another boy you had never seen, in handcuffs. You know how you would feel about it. You would be sorry for the other boy, but you did not know him; but with your own boy, your grief would penetrate your heart like a sword. For only love can grieve. If those two boys were sent off to prison, you might pity the boy you did not know, but you would grieve over the boy you did know.

The mother can grieve because she loves. If you do not love, you cannot grieve. Therefore, when the scripture says, "Grieve not the Holy Spirit of God," it is telling us that He loves us so much that when we insult Him, He is grieved. When we ignore Him, He is grieved; when we resist Him, He is grieved; when we doubt Him, He is grieved.

In like manner, we can please Him by obeying and believing. When we please Him, He responds to us just as a pleased father responds, just as a pleased mother responds. He will respond to us because He is pleased, because He loves us.

If we were to increase our attendance until there wasn't a place to put them, if we were to get $10,000 or $20,000 given to us, if we were to have anything that men want and love and put value on without the Holy Spirit, you might as well have nothing at all. For "This is the word of the LORD unto Zerubbabel, saying, Not by might, nor by power, but by my Spirit, saith the LORD of hosts" (Zechariah 4:6). Not by the eloquence of a man, not by good music, not by good preaching, but it is by the Spirit that God works His mighty work.

We had better throw ourselves back on God, for there will be a day when we will have nothing but God.

What is the Spirit? Who is the Spirit? How do we know who the Spirit is? We know by the Scriptures. We know because the Church Fathers knew what the Scriptures said. Unless He is feelingly in our midst, unless He is consciously in our midst, He might as well be somewhere else. It is possible to run a church without the Holy Spirit, which is the terrible thing. You organize it. You get a board, a pastor, a choir, a ladies aid society and a Sunday school, and you get all organized. I believe in organization. I am not against it, I am for it. You get organized, and you get a pastor to turn the crank, and that is all there is to it. The Holy Ghost can leave, and the pastor goes on turning the crank, and nobody finds it out for five years. Oh, what a horrible tragedy to the Church of Christ.

But, we do not have to have it that way. This kind of preaching is going to do one of two things. There is going to be a reaction from it, or, there is going to be an eager seeking. I'm praying and believing the latter will be the case. I believe that there will be an eager seeking for better things than that we now have.

God's Word to the church today is the restoration of the Spirit to His rightful place in the Church, and in your life is, by all means, the most important that could possibly take place.

## CHAPTER 2

# Promise of the Father

THE FATHER PROMISED THE SPIRIT as a gift to His children. I do not know if this is right or not, but I think maybe God had in mind the love people have for their children. He did say, "If ye then, being evil, know how to give good gifts unto your children, how much more shall your Father which is in heaven give good things to them that ask him?" (Matthew 7:11). In making the Spirit the promise of the Father, I wonder if He did not want to show that you do not have to be afraid of the Holy Spirit?

It is quite difficult to get a Christian over the fear of the Holy Spirit. By that, I do not mean reverence for Him. You cannot reverence the Holy Spirit too much, but you can be afraid of Him. I am sure many people are afraid of the Holy Spirit. But if you could remember, He is the Father's promise, given to us as the promised gift. Just as a man promises his son a bicycle for Christmas, and the boy remembers and comes back and reminds the father. Nobody is ever afraid of a promise of a father who loves him.

The members of the redeemed Church should be bound in the bundle of love for the Holy Spirit. The truth is, God never thought of His church apart from the Holy Spirit. We were born of the Spirit. We are baptized into the body of Christ by the Spirit. We are anointed with the Spirit. We are led of the Spirit. We are taught of the Spirit, and the Spirit is the medium, the divine solution, in which God holds His church. The hymnist portrayed the Holy Spirit as the "essence of the godhead uncreated." God never dreamed of His people apart from the Holy Spirit, and accordingly made promises to them.

Let us note some promises He made.

He said, for instance, "Until the spirit be poured upon us from on high, and the wilderness be a fruitful field, and the fruitful field be counted for a forest. Then judgment shall dwell in the wilderness, and righteousness remain in the fruitful field. And the work of righteousness shall be peace; and the effect of righteousness, quietness, and assurance for ever." (Isaiah 32:15-17).

Further on in Isaiah, He says, "For I will pour water upon him that is thirsty, and floods upon the dry ground: I will pour my spirit upon thy seed, and my blessing upon thine offspring:" (Isaiah 44:3).

Then consider that famous passage in Joel, "And it shall come to pass afterward, that I will pour out my spirit upon all flesh; and your sons and your daughters shall prophesy, your old men shall dream dreams, your young men shall see visions: And also upon the servants and upon the handmaids in those days will I pour out my Spirit" (Joel 2:28-29).

Now, those are the words of the Father, and Jesus interpreted these words and called them the promise of the Father. Stay close by the interpretation whenever our Lord interprets the Old Testament. Do not depend too much or lean too hard on the interpretations of man, because we can be wrong. But our Lord, the Man Christ Jesus, never was. He called this the "promise of the Father." That is, the Father, through the years, had made a promise and now Jesus sums it up and calls it the "promise of the Father." He says, "And, behold, I send the promise of my Father upon you: but tarry ye in the city of Jerusalem, until ye be endued with power from on high," (Luke 24:49).

In John 14–16, you will find our Lord talking about the Holy Spirit and His coming to the Church. In the Church, in the Gospels, in Acts and over into the Epistles there are three periods that are discernible with respect to the Holy Spirit and His work in the Church.

## PERIOD OF PROMISE
There is the period of the Promise. That is from John the Baptist to the resurrection of Christ. The marks of this three-year period include the disciples being called, commissioned and taught. If we could get together a congregation as spiritual as the disciples were before Pentecost, we would consider we had a very spiritual church. We would make bishops out of them. We would elect them to the boards and would write their lives and name churches after them, if we could find somebody just as spiritual as they were before the Holy Ghost came at Pentecost.

Many refer to these disciples as ignorant. Do you know these disciples had three years in the best Bible school in the world? There is not a seminary on earth that can equal the seminary with Jesus as the whole faculty. He was teaching them, instructing them, and sitting with them.

A university once consisted of Mark Hopkins on one end of a log and a boy on the other. A Bible school consists of our Lord Jesus Christ and a willing student. The disciples went to the best Bible school in the world. Now, they did not get a degree they could frame and put on their study wall, but they had a degree inside them. They loved Christ our Lord, living and dead and living again.

That was the period of the promise when they had not received anything yet. They only had been promised something. All this time until His death and even after, Jesus was creating expectation in them. He was telling them that there was a new kind of life coming to them. A life that was not to be poetic, psychic, or physical, but it was to be an afflatus from above. It was to be something to come to them out of the world beyond them, over the threshold of their beings into the sanctum sanatorium, into the pentralia, into the deep of their spirit. There He would live and teach them and lead them, making them holy and giving them power. Jesus taught that all the way through.

Wherever He could find a time, and the people were about Him and the circumstances were good, He would tell them these things. And as they came nearer to the end of His earthly life, He intensified this teaching. He told them that there was a new and superior kind of life coming. It was to be an infusion, an outpouring of spiritual energy. Then He left them.

## PERIOD OF PREPARATION

The second period was the period of preparation. Of course, in some measure they were being prepared while He walked with them. After He had gone, they then began to prepare. They stopped their activities. You know what is the matter with us in our day? We are the busiest bunch of eager beavers I have ever known or have ever been, probably, in the religious world. The idea is that if you are not running in a circle, if you're not breathing down the back of your own neck, you are not pleasing God.

When the Lord said, "Go ye into all the world and preach the gospel to every creature," Peter leaped to his feet and scooped up his hat on his way out. He was going to go right now. He was anxious to go out and found something or start something. But the Lord said, "Peter, tarry ye in the city of Jerusalem until ye be endued with power from on high."

I think a big mistake we make with our young people is, as soon as they are converted to Christ, we start them out right away in some Christian activity. My brethren, we are not prepared to do the work of the Lord when we are just born-again. The priest was born a priest but had to be anointed before serving. They had to be born of the tribe of Levi of the family of Aaron. They had to be born into the priesthood or they could not be priests. However, they did not serve until they had been anointed. Blood was put on their ears, on their thumbs, on their toes. And then on the blood was put oil, fragrant, sweet oil; a type of the Holy Ghost. After being anointed, they went to serve in the Old Testament priesthood.

But just as soon as a young person is born-again, we give him a bunch of tracts and say, "Now, Bud, get going." And the result is Christianity has taken on the spirit of amateurism. I heard a former president of Wheaton College once say Christianity is suffering a rash of amateurism. And he was right, we surely are.

Christianity has levelled down and the high quality is gone. We are as light as butterflies. We flit around in the sunshine, imagining we are eagles flapping our broad wings above the rocks of God. Instead of that, we are butterflies. We are trying to work when we are not prepared to work.

I have said the church would be better off if we called for a moratorium on activity for about six weeks, and just wait on God to see what He would do for us. Just wait on God. The early church did that very thing. They cleaned up the loose ends and were united.

We pray, "Oh, God, send Thy Holy Spirit upon us so we'll be united." We might just as well repeat "Three Blind Mice." God does not hear that kind of prayer because it has no sense in it. The Holy Ghost did not come upon the disciples to unite them. The Holy Spirit came upon the disciples because they were already united, "Being of one accord and in one place."

Scholars tell us that "being of one accord" is a musical term, meaning harmony. The early Christians already were one. They were in harmony with each other when they were together in one place.

The trouble with some is that they are here, but not all here. Their mind is wandering around all over the place, but they are here in body. The disciples were together in one place.

Someone said that we have yet to see what God can do with a man if He can get him together in one place.

## PERIOD OF REALIZATION

Then came the third period, the period of realization. The Holy Ghost came upon them suddenly. It was not until just lately that I noticed a word here in the book of Acts, the word "suddenly." "And suddenly there came a sound from heaven as of a rushing mighty wind, and it filled all the house where they were sitting," (Acts 2:2).

I smile to myself, because of that word "suddenly." God's people are so afraid of "suddenly." They always want things to slip up on them a little bit at a time, slowly. Everybody is willing to be filled with the Holy Spirit provided God does it very gingerly and slowly, and does not take away their face nor embarrass them nor frighten them. But the scripture says, "Suddenly they were filled with the Holy Ghost." It even says, "Suddenly there was with the angel a multitude of the heavenly hosts." I think you will find that word occurring whenever God did a wonderful thing. He did it suddenly.

We are afraid of that. We want to grow in grace, because you can grow without embarrassment. If an altar call is given, and you go to the prayer room and get down on your knees and seek Almighty God, and God comes and fills you, and you get up and get your handkerchief out and daub your eyes and say, "Thank God the Comforter has come." It is embarrassing. It takes a little bit away from your reputation. You got a feeling, "Look at me, I used to be the chairman of the board and I taught a Sunday school class, now for me to suddenly be filled with the Spirit and maybe even break down and cry or say, 'Praise the Lord'... It would be awful."

The result is we go on year after year, and learn to live with death. We learn to live with a spiritual corpse. We learn to live with our breath frosty and our cheeks pale, our toes frostbitten, without spirituality; yet we learn to live with that. We imagine that is normal. We write books to prove it is normal. It is not normal at all. It is subnormal, abnormal, below normal. The Holy Ghost is not on us and that is our trouble.

The period of the realization came suddenly, and the Father fulfilled His promise and the expectations were fully met and more. Always remember this: God is always bigger than anything God can say, because words are inadequate to express God and what God can do. Any promise God ever made, God has to fulfill it. The reason being, God is so great, His heart so kind and His desire so intense and tremendous that language does not express it. Not the Greek, not the English, no language expresses God. It cannot. If language could contain God then language would be equal to God.

So everything God says in the Bible must be understood to be a little greater than what He says, even as God is greater than language. God promised them that they should receive power and that power should be an afflatus from heaven above, which should come upon them; should cross the threshold of their spirits and enter the depths of their soul and dwell there forever, and should work within them, lead them, purify them, instruct them, teach them. We have to believe that the fulfilments will be greater than the promise, because the fulfilment of God and the promise are mere words.

I was at a convention in New York State, where a beautiful little Italian woman was in the audience. I preached from the Old Testament text that says, "What prayer and supplication soever be made by any man, or by all thy people Israel, which shall know every man the plague of his own heart, and spread forth his hands toward this house:"(1 Kings 8:38). I preached on the "Plague of a man's heart." I told them there was deliverance, there was a "balm in Gilead" and there was a "fountain opened in the house of David" to deliver us from the plague of our own heart. She, along with some others, came down to the altar.

Suddenly, she leaped to her feet; no wildness, no wild and woolly stuff. It was God. That lovely dark face of hers literally shown and she walked around saying, "Oh, I didn't know it could happen to me. I didn't know it could happen to me."

She made a dash for an older man, threw her arms around him and hugged him hard. They had a little word together and then she turned away all tears and smiles. I learned afterward it was her father-in-law. They had a little quibble and she was just hugging him and making up, which is perfectly normal and right.

That is the fulfilment. She read it in the text and heard it preached; but what happened to her was so much greater than anything she had dreamed of, she could not believe it was happening, but it happened all right.

I am not one of these positive preachers. A preacher is supposed to be positive, to accent the positive and underplay the negative. Everybody who knows how to screw in a light bulb knows there are two poles in an electric circuit. The positive and the negative and you cannot have a light burning on one. It takes both. Everybody knows there are two sides to a dollar. Spilt it down the middle and there is no store anywhere who would take it. Both sides have to be there, the positive and the negative. There must be the negative, you have to get rid of some things.

I never had any time for these soft-handed, cake-eating pastors who look more normal with a teacup balanced on their knee then they do on their knees in the study. I never could see it, but they walk around smooth and sweet, hoping never to make any enemies as long as they live. Brother, a man is known by the enemies he makes and by the friends he makes. I want God's friends to be my friends, and I am not so particular about God's enemies whether they are my friends or not. I do not want to be friends of those that are enemies of God.

Sometimes I have to tear into things I do not believe are right. I would not do it except it hinders the people of God.

Anything that hinders God's people is my business, so do not say, "That's none of your business." I have been anointed by God to make it my business.

I heard an error abroad all my life. It is stated like this: the individual Christian is not affected by this promise of the Father. This happened to the Church once and is not to be repeated. Just as the birth of Christ happened once, and is not to be repeated. The death of Christ happened once, and is not to be repeated. The resurrection of Christ happened once, and is not to be repeated. Therefore, Pentecost happened once and the Church is no longer concerned that that has taken place. And so they try to brush us off.

I am going to ask some questions now, and let you do your own preaching. You will have made your own decision about it. I have got about six questions I want to ask you, and you answer them.

The first question is, was the Father's promise for the first century Christians only? This promise of the Father that was to come, was that for the first century Christians only? Or, did that carry over to the second, third and fourth centuries?

My early theological education came out of the Scofield Bible. Scofield says the period Joel had in mind when he says, "it shall come to pass in the last days that I will pour out my spirit upon all flesh," began at Pentecost and continues until Christ returns. We are living in the period of the last days when that text of Joel is active, efficacious and applicable to you and me.

I quote Dr. Scofield because often he is quoted as not being on the side of the Spirit-filled life, but he was an honest man and said that, "we are now living in those latter days when God will pour out His Spirit upon all flesh." That is what he believed.

Dr. R. A. Torrey said, "When Peter said 'believe on the Lord Jesus Christ and receive the gift of the Spirit which the promise is unto you and to your children and to as many as are far off,' it was not for that first generation only. You and your children and as many as are far off "

That is the first question. Now you settle it, brother. If I try to make you believe something you will go away and if you meet a man that is a better arguer than I am, he will make you believe the opposite. That is always the reason why I believe in the witness of the Spirit. If you can argue a man into believing he is filled, he will meet another man that will argue him out of being filled. If you can argue a young fellow into thinking he is born again, he will meet someone who will argue him out of it. So, I never argue with anybody. I point to the Lamb of God that taketh away the sin of the world, and after that God and the man are on their own. Then, if I drop dead or get hit by a Volkswagen, he will have the promise of the Father. He will not have to go back to me to find out whether it is so or not.

The second question, does the new birth of the first century Christians make my new birth unnecessary?

The Lord said that we would have to be born again and we were to be filled with the Spirit. Now they come along and tell us that meant they were to be filled with the Spirit back there. All right, grant they were filled with the Spirit. But I happened to be born a few hundred years too late for that first century. Here I am high and dry, hanging on a wire. If I did not live back then I am finished, I do not have any hope at all.

I will not listen to that kind of teaching. Does Peter being born again do it for me? Peter was filled with the Spirit, then does Peter being filled with the Spirit do for me?

Would a breakfast that Peter ate in 30 A.D. nourish me today? Peter ate his breakfast and was nourished in 30 A.D. I am living now and I have to have my breakfast. I have to eat now if I am going to be nourished now. Peter being born again will not help me today. I must be born again now as he was born again then. Peter being filled that day will not help me now; I must be filled now as he was filled then. Is there any difference between that and the outpouring of the Spirit?

Another question, what is it to the church in Toronto that the church in Jerusalem was filled with the Holy Ghost. Sometimes it seems to me that the Lord's people need to have somebody gently rub their heads. They get such weird ideas. They need something to shake their head and get it working. This idea that the church being filled with the Spirit back there in the first century made it unnecessary for the church to be filled now.

How silly can you get? None of us was living in the first century. I wasn't. Nobody I know around here was. We were not even in the minds of our great grandfathers yet. Some of you are so proud of your ancestry. As the brother said in the House of Lords in London, "You were eating acorns in the forests of Brittany back there at that time." I do not know where my ancestors were, in the black forests of Germany somewhere, I guess, digging roots. But way back of that is the hour when the Holy Ghost came upon the Church. The Church went out in a blaze of fire to preach the gospel to the world in the first hundred years.

They also insist that at conversion we receive what they received back there at Pentecost. I want to ask you, have you ever seen anybody that received at his conversion what Peter received in the upper chamber? Have you ever met anybody like that? Do you know anybody like that? When you were converted, did you have the power Peter had when he preached? Didn't the average Christian in the early Church have something that apparently we do not have in this day? I think they did.

Is modern fundamentalism a satisfactory fulfilment of expectation raised by the Father and Christ? Our heavenly Father promised the gift of the Holy Ghost to come upon His children. Jesus promised that we should have the Spirit, that He would come. He should take the things of Christ and make them known unto us. He should bring all things to our memory. We should have power when the Spirit came. He promised all this, and I look around at cold, dead, dry-up fundamentalism. Textualism hanging out to dry. Then they want me to believe that what they have is what they had back then. I just cannot do it. We Christians now are a scrub lot compared to those Christians back there.

Then, does your heart, personally, witness that what you now enjoy is what our Lord promised to His people? Does your heart now bear witness that what you now have is all that God meant when He painted that wonderful picture of the fullness of the Spirit? Or, is there something more for the Church?

Somebody wants to ask the question, now. "We don't know this man Tozer. What is he? Is this Pentecostalism? Is he preaching tongues?" No, absolutely not. It is only what the Christian and Missionary Alliance has always believed. It is only what Dr. R. A. Torrey believed. It is what Billy Sunday believed. It is what Billy Graham believes, although Billy was gifted of God to preach to sinners. He does not enter this too much because his gift is different and he preaches straight to sinners. It is what D. L. Moody believed.

Years ago on the Southside of the city of Chicago, there was a little home. In the home lived an elderly woman full of the Holy Ghost named Mother Cook. A young fellow was converted in the city and he would have made a good salesman. He was very busy. He loved to run in circles. He went everywhere running in circles. His name was Dwight Lyman Moody. One day Mother Cook saw Dwight and said, "Son, I would like you to come over to my house sometime. I want to talk to you."

Moody went over to her house. She sat him down on a chair and said, "Now, Dwight. It is wonderful to see you saved so beautifully. It is wonderful to see you so zealous. But do you know what you need? You need to be anointed with the Holy Ghost."

"Well," Moody said. "I want everything God has for me."

"All right," she said, "get down here." He got down on the linoleum and they prayed awhile. She prayed, "Oh, God, fill this young fellow." Moody died out there, opened his heart, brought his empty vessel to the Lord and took the promise by faith, but nothing happened.

A few days afterward, he was in Philadelphia. He said, "As I was walking down the street suddenly God fulfilled the promise He had made to me in that kitchen." And down on him came a horn of oil and the Holy Ghost came on him. He said he crawled up an alley and raised his hand and prayed, "Oh God, stay your power or I'll die." Then he said, "I went out from there preaching the same sermons with the same texts but oh, the difference now." The Holy Ghost had come. Now, the Holy Ghost had been there. He had caused him to be born again. "If any man have not the Spirit of Christ he is none of His."

It is one thing to have the Spirit as my Regenerator and quite a different thing to have the horn of oil poured out on my head. The reason I can talk about it with a good deal of authority is I went through it and I know what I am preaching about. I did not learn this at any seminary. The Holy Ghost did this. God did this, so I am giving it to you.

You ponder these things. There is not any use to try to push you into anything. When you push God's poor children around the result is we get many weird monstrosities instead of saints. I do not want to do that. I want you to set aside some time, search the scriptures and see whether these things are so.

Some people say they are not so. Some people say that all I am doing is confusing people. I wrote a series of articles for a magazine on the Holy Spirit and a fellow has been after me since. He published things about me showing that I am confusing the saints.

I wrote him a letter and said, "My dear brother, if the Lord's people were as eager to be filled with the Spirit as they are to prove they can't be, the Church would be quite a different church." He published that, too. But, it is true.

I am not preaching a thing that our Baptist brethren do not believe when you press them. I am not preaching a thing that the Methodist brethren do not believe. I am not preaching a thing that the Salvation Army does not teach. I am not preaching a thing that our Puritan Fathers did not believe. Therefore, I do not apologize.

Set aside time and search the Scriptures. And if the Scriptures do not convince you that the Church and the individuals in the Church ought to be living a happy, Spirit-filled life, then do not listen to me. Because if I preach five hours straight and I do not preach according to the truth found in the Bible, I am wrong no matter how eloquent I try to be. Pray, yield, believe, obey and see what God will do for you over the next weeks.

## CHAPTER 3

# What Difference Does the Holy Spirit Make?

OUR LORD TOLD HIS DISCIPLES they had a huge job before them: to preach the gospel to every creature, to go everywhere throughout the world and tell them that they could be saved by faith in Jesus Christ. Yet He forbade them to go immediately. He said, "You are to go," and when they started, He said, "Now, don't go." There must have been a compelling reason for His telling them to wait.

Right here let me tell you a little trick people have. It is the neatest little trick imaginable for getting out of tight spot when it comes to the necessity for being filled with the Spirit. We push conversion down and make it to be less to make room for the deeper work of grace. Then, when we get the deeper work of grace, we do not have any more than our old Baptist and Presbyterian and Methodist Fathers had when they had their initial experience of being born again.

I do not want to do that. I do not want to make sinners out of these disciples so that I might later make room for their being converted. That is a good way to dodge, but, brother and sister, one of these days you and I will be where dodges will not work. We had better not dodge now; we should face up to things while we can.

Now, who were these to whom Jesus spoke?

They were His called and chosen disciples. They possessed and had received divine authority. They had an authority that very few people now would dare to try to exercise. He said, "Go everywhere; and when you go, cast out the devils, and heal the sick, and take all my authority." He gave it to these people. He did not give His authority to people who had no spiritual experience. You can be sure of that. The persons to whom Jesus said, "tarry until ye be endued with power" knew Jesus Christ in a warm, intimate way. They knew Him living, they knew Him dead, and then they knew Him living again. They had been with Him three years and over. Then they had seen Him die on a cross, and then they had seen Him after He had risen from the dead. So they knew Him living, dead and living again. They had shown evidence of being truly converted persons.

Some people say they were converted when the Spirit came upon them at Pentecost. I do not believe that at all. It is a modern twist people have given doctrine to make room for their cold carnality. They had shown evidence of being truly converted men and Christ had declared them so. Now if you doubt that, let me read the prayer that Jesus made about these disciples. He prayed "For I have given unto them the words which thou gavest me; and they have received them, and have known surely that I came out from thee, and they have believed that thou didst send me" (John 17:8).

Then He said in verse 14, "I have given them thy word; and the world hath hated them, because they are not of the world, even as I am not of the world" (John 17:1).

These were the things Jesus said to His Father about His disciples He had gathered around Him there. Surely, that did not sound like the Lord talking about sinners.

Christ outlined for them a program of world evangelization and told them in Acts, "But ye shall receive power, after that the Holy Ghost is come upon you: and ye shall be witnesses unto me both in Jerusalem, and in all Judaea, and in Samaria, and unto the uttermost part of the earth" (Acts 1:8).

He said they were to enter a new era. We are always praying for revival. What is praying for revival? What do we hope to have when we have a revival? I do not know what some people want, but I suppose generally we are hoping to enter a new spiritual era. God was to introduce a change of dispensation, but He was not to introduce a change of dispensation apart from a stepped up and elevated spiritual experience.

The Lord does not have calendars that He pulls off a January and puts up a February, and shifts and change dispensationally like that. He has dispensations, but those dispensations have to do with people, not with calendars. They have to do with spiritual experience, not with calendars. So when they were to enter a new era it was not only to be a change over from one dispensation to another. It was to be introduced by a coming down of a new afflatus from above. Something was to come that had not been there before. And it was to enter them and possess them. It was to bring God to them in a way He was not with them then, and was to enter them and dwell there.

That is the difference between Christianity and all of the oriental cults and occult religions. The occult religions try to wake up what you already have. Christianity says, what you have isn't enough; I'm going to send an enduement from above that shall enter you and be to you what you lack. There is the difference.

They say, "Wake up your solar plexus," which is one religion. I do not even know where mine is. I could not even locate the thing. Then they say, "Stir up the thing that is in you." What is the use? If there were four or five lions coming, you could not say to a little French poodle, "Wake up the lion in you." That would not work. They would chew the poor little fellow up and swallow him, haircut and all, because a French poodle just is not sufficient for the lion. If God wanted a French poodle to fight a lion, He would have to put the heart and body of the lion in the poodle. He would have to make him bigger and stronger than his opponent.

That is exactly what the Holy Spirit says He does. But the occult religion says, concentrate and free your mind and release the creative powers that lie in you and you will be all right. The simple fact is creative powers do not lie in us. We begin to die the moment we are born.

You and I do not have hidden potentials, creative impulses, and all that kind of stuff in us. We walk around on the earth barely able to keep going. As we get older, the gravitational pull slowly drags us down and humps us over. Finally, we give up one day with a sigh and go back to Mother Earth. That is the kind of potential we have. We have the potential to be a corpse. God Almighty says, "I do not want to wake up the power that lies in you. Ye shall receive the power of the Holy Spirit coming upon you." That is a different thing altogether, my friend.

If we only need to be awakened, the Lord would simply have gone around waking us up. But we needed more than just to be awakened. We need to be endued with power from on high.

They were to enter a new era and it was to mark something grandly new and an enriched spiritual condition. What difference did this make? What difference did it make to these disciples?

Let me point out some things it did not do. We must rule out as evidence all the blessings they had before. Because, obviously anything they had before, the Spirit did not bring when He came.

For instance, they were true disciples and they had a consciousness of true discipleship. They were the Lord's own loving disciples. That did not come at Pentecost. That had been before. They were converted and forgiven and had fellowship with Christ and they had something a lot of people, even ministers, now do not have. They had the gift of preaching and went around everywhere preaching. And they had power to work miracles. Such a power that they came back saying, "Lord, even the devils are under our power when we go out." The Lord told them to be glad their names were written in heaven. He did not say they did not have the power. He knew they did. He gave it to them.

Some say that if you are filled with the Spirit you will have a miracle, forgetting they had miracles before they were filled with the Spirit.

As I shall try to show, the power of the Holy Spirit is not necessary to make miracle workers. The power of the Holy Spirit is something infinitely higher, grander and more wonderful than that. They worked miracles before the Spirit ever came.

## WHAT DIFFERENCE DID THE HOLY SPIRIT MAKE?

Here were the disciples in the book of John. Then there was a sudden change and the disciples were in the book of Acts and spilled over into the epistles and Revelation. What difference was there? Was there a difference? There was a time when they were pre-Pentecost then came the outpouring of the Spirit and they were post-Pentecost. What was the difference?

Let me point out seven things the Holy Spirit did for them. I believe in searching the Scripture to see if these things are true. And if they are true, amen and if not then it would make no difference who said they were. I could get up here and talk from now until the end of this century, and if I were not preaching according to the Scripture there would not be a bit of truth in what I have said.

The first is a sudden brilliant consciousness of God being actually present. They had this. They knew Jesus and loved Jesus; but now, when the Holy Spirit came upon them, they had a sudden consciousness; brilliant consciousness of God being actually present. A veil was raised and they felt God. A sense of acute God-consciousness was on them from that time on. They knew themselves to be in immediate contact with another world.

My brethren, that is exactly what the average Gospel church does not have today. We are not in contact with another world. We are very happily in contact with this world. But those disciples were other-worldly. Many liberals have made fun of that hyphenated expression "other-worldly." They say, "You are so everlastingly good you are no good. You are so heavenly you are no good on earth."

The day will come when God will judge every man out of his own mouth. I believe in being other-worldly. That is, I believe that a sense of God and heaven ought to be upon us. We ought to live in that. Day by day whether we are businessmen or farmers or schoolteachers or whatever we are, we ought to have this sense of heaven upon us.

I can tell you that only the Holy Spirit can give, bring, impart and maintain that sense of the divine presence. There was a sudden freshness of seeing and hearing and feeling that came on these disciples. As if, a cloud had been rolled back and the city of God, before unsuspected and unseen, now suddenly became clearly visible before their eyes. There was a word that entered then, found in the book of Acts, the word wonder. So they wondered. The word "wonder" occurred so much.

The church these days does not have any sense of wonder. Have you noticed that? No sense of wonderment. You can explain everything. There is a constant note of joyous surprise in the book of Acts and on over in the epistles. They were being surprised by God. There was a note of wonder; they were amazed at what God was doing. He was blessing them to the point where He was amazing them.

One dear man said, "God is so good to me that it scares me. God is so good to me that it amazes me and frightens me." That is what I mean. That came to these disciples and it is a spirit, a quality that lies upon them from that time on.

The second difference the Holy Spirit made was He gave them the joy of the Holy Ghost. That is, a change of emotional tone came at once. In the Four Gospels, there is not too much joy. There is instruction and a lot of subdued and quiet joy, or at least peace. However, there is not the joy there. When we get over into the book of Acts, it changes from the minor key into the major. Have you ever heard the old Jewish songs sung in a minor key? I like to hear them. They are somewhat sad and gloomy, and if you sing them long enough I suppose you would break down. The point is that they are joyless. They groan, moan, plead and long, but they never arrive at anything.

I am thinking about God's dear people always praying for joy and praying for light and praying for every benediction, and yet they do not get it. They want to pray for it Sunday all day long and then Sunday night go home and sigh, and go to bed and give up, and come back and do the same thing over again. The nearest thing that illustrates that is a story the old Greeks told.

In Greek mythology, old Zeus punished Sisyphus by sending him to limbo or whatever kind of hell the Greeks had. Here is what he had to do throughout eternity. They gave him a great big rock and told him to roll it to the top of the hill. He rolled it, sweating and struggling and pushing and bruising his shoulder. He rolled the rock up within an inch or two of the top and just when he got near the top, he slipped and fell. The rock rolled back to the bottom and he had to go back and do it all over again. He would have that to do through eternity as a punishment for his sin.

The fellow who thought that out had a little preview of hell, for the frustration, the disappointment, the labor without reward that must be there. Surely, they must have had some vision of hell. But I hate to think that it gets among the Christians. We ought to know better. Christians work themselves up Sunday, then go back down, and start all over on a lower level on Monday. Perhaps they work themselves up a little on Wednesday night, but the point is, it never seems to stick. The bell loses its clapper. It does not ring any more.

The happiness of these disciples was the happiness of the Holy Ghost. God sang, and the Scripture says that we are to be filled with the Spirit singing. Singing and making melody in your hearts unto the Lord. Choirs ought not to sing for churches, they ought to sing for the Lord and let the church hear. That is the way it is when the Holy Ghost is in control. We are to be filled with the Holy Ghost, singing unto the Lord, and the people hear. Then they are blessed while we sing unto the Lord.

The happiness of these people was not the happiness of Adam. It was not the happiness of nature. When we try to work nature up to happiness, a child can be happy.

We work up a joy of some sort. We try to get joy in our hearts and we try it in dance halls, in rock and roll sessions. I do not own a TV but when I am around a hotel, I look at one. I have seen some of those young people rocking and rolling and I never saw a happy face yet. They seem to be in a cold trance of some sort. That is the effort to work Adam up into joy. Adam is not basically happy because Adam has to die and go back to earth again, and go to hell unless he is converted through the blood. The human race is anything but happy, so we work ourselves up.

The joy of the Holy Ghost is not worked up. The joy of the Holy Ghost is that which comes to the heart. It is a post-resurrection joy. You see, Christ came out of the grave and the Spirit of the Risen Christ comes back to His people; and the joy we have is the joy that looks back on death, not the joy that we have in spite of the fact we have to die. But the joy we have is a result of the fact that, in Christ, we already died and rose, and there is no death out there for the true child of God.

There was the joy of the Holy Ghost and there is the third, the power of their words to penetrate and arrest. I do not have to tell you there is a difference between the penetrating power of words. Even the same words and the same sentence spoken by one man will put you under conviction, spoken by another man leaves you completely cold. The Holy Spirit makes that difference. He said, "Ye shall be endued with power," and the word power there means the ability to do.

When Peter preached at Pentecost, they were stricken in their hearts when they heard him. They were pierced, stricken through in their hearts and they said, "Men and brethren, what shall we do?"

If you will look at the second chapter of Acts, you will see what it says there. They were pricked in their hearts and said unto Peter, "Men and brethren, what shall we do?"

## THAT PRICKING IN THEIR HEART

When it says in the Gospel of John that the soldier pierced the heart of Jesus, the word used, pierced, is not as strong a word as the word pricked. It is a stronger word in the original. In other words, the words of Peter at Pentecost went further into the hearts of the hearers then the spear went into the heart of Jesus. The word is a stronger word, not in English but in Greek. The Holy Spirited penetrated, and that is one of the works of the Holy Spirit. He comes and penetrates; He sharpens the point of the arrows of the man of God.

D. L. Moody said he preached the same sermons after he was filled with the Spirit. "I didn't change sermons but, what a difference." Moody had the power that penetrated. Before he simply tried to reason with people, beg them and coax them to

59

come. Now a divine penetration went straight through, passed their reasoning power into their heart.

They had, fourth, a clear sense of the reality of everything. You noticed that in the Four Gospels, they were asking questions and in the book of Acts, they were answering questions. That is the difference. That is the difference between a Spirit-filled man and one that is not. The man of God, the preacher that is not Spirit-filled makes a great deal, and one of his phrases is likely to be "and now let us ask ourselves this question." Have you ever heard this from the pulpit? I have often wondered why the reverend wanted to ask himself a question. Why didn't he settle that at home before he came to church? Always asking questions. "And, now, what shall we say?"

Brother, God never put a preacher in the pulpit to ask questions; he put a preacher in the pulpit to answer questions. He put him there with authority to stand up in the name of God to speak and answer questions. Back in the Gospels, they were always asking questions. "Lord, shall it be? Lord how shall it be? Lord, who? Lord, what?" But when they got to the book of Acts, they began to answer questions. And they stood with authority. The same Peter that sneaked around, warmed his hand at the world's fire, and lied to the little woman that recognized his accent. He was standing boldly to preach the word of the Lord. That was the difference. There was authority there. That is our trouble.

I know there ought to be a lot more authority in the pulpit than there is. A preacher ought to reign from the pulpit as a king from his throne. Not by law, not by regulations, or not by board meetings and annual meetings only, although I believe in them too. He ought to by moral ascendancy. When a man of God stands to speak, he ought to have the authority of God on him so he makes the people responsible to listen to him. When they do not listen to him, they are accountable to God for turning down the divine word. Instead of that, we have a lot of tabby-cats with their claws carefully trimmed in the seminary. They can paw over their congregations and never scratch them at all. They have had their claws trimmed. They are just as soft and sweet.

I believe in the authority of God. And I believe if a man does not have it, he ought to go away somewhere and wait until he gets the authority. Then stand up to speak if he has to begin by preaching on a soapbox on a street corner or go to a rescue mission and preach with authority. They had it in those days. When they stood up, there was authority there.

Then, a sharp separation between them and the world. I suppose I ought to skip that. On their part, they were seeing another world. They were looking at another world. They really saw another world. Nowadays, evangelical Christianity is trying to convert this world to the Church. Bringing it in, head over heels, world and all. Unregenerated, uncleansed, unshriven, unbaptised, unsanctified ... bringing the world right into the church. If you can just get a big-shot to say something nice about the church, they rush into print, usually in bad English, and tell about this fellow. What nice things he said. I do not give a hoot about big-shots because I serve a living Savior and Jesus Christ is Lord of lords and King of kings. He picked up a farm boy from the hills of Pennsylvania, anointed my head with oil and said, "Go out and tell them."

And I have been telling them. I do not care whether people listen, but they will know a prophet has been among them. I believe every man ought to have this authority, this separation, that will make him see another world. If there is any converting, it is going to be a one-way street. The world is going to come to us; we are not going to the world.

Then another thing; they took a great delight in prayer. The only one who could stay awake praying in the Gospels was Jesus. Others tried to pray but they came to Him and said, "Teach us to pray." But He knew you could not teach anybody to pray. They are giving courses on how to pray, today. How ridiculous. It is like giving a course on how to fall in love. No, when the Holy Spirit comes, He takes the things of God and translates them into language our hearts understand. Even if we do not know the will of God, the Holy Ghost does, and He prays with groanings that cannot be uttered. These disciples were praying people. They were always praying somewhere, always off somewhere praying. Before that, they would fall asleep. Now, nobody was sleeping. They had a great delight in prayer.

And a passionate love for the Scriptures. This is the seventh thought. Did you know that Jesus quoted the Scriptures in the Gospels but the disciples quoted the Scriptures in the Acts? There was the difference.

I remember a dear saint of God who said once, years ago, "When I was filled with the Spirit I loved the Scriptures so much that if I could have gotten more of the word inside me by eating it I would have eaten the book, leather and everything, if I could have gotten more of the book inside my heart." You do not get it by eating it, although Ezekiel was told to eat the roll. And so the woman had some Scriptural authority for what she said.

But, the word of God is sweet to the Spirit-filled person because the Spirit wrote the Scriptures. You cannot read the Scriptures with the spirit of Adam, for the Spirit of God inspired them. The spirit of the world does not appreciate the Scriptures. It is the Spirit of God that appreciates the Scriptures. One little flash of the Holy Ghost will give you more inward divine illumination on the meaning of the text then all the commentators that ever commentated. Yet I have commentaries. I am not talking against things. I am only trying to show you that if you have everything and have not the fullness of the Holy Ghost, you are nothing. When you have the Holy Spirit, then God may use anything and everything. He uses boards and ladies praying groups and commentators and all the rest.

But we try to get along without the Holy Spirit and that is the terrible thing. How different it is today, the contrast. We live by hearsay. A vague sense of reality and wonder is missing.

The Moravians were just quiet people like you and me. But they waited one morning and suddenly, as they waited and prepared their hearts, something came which they called a "sense of the loving nearness of the Savior instantaneously bestowed."

When the Holy Spirit is allowed, and when He does have particular intimacy with the human soul, He never talks about Himself; He talks about the Lord Jesus Christ for He came to reveal Jesus.

The Holy Ghost fell on that Moravian crowd in 1727. They did not say a sense of the loving nearness of the Spirit, but a sense of the loving nearness of the Savior instantaneously bestowed. Zinzendorf said, "That group of seventy-five German Christians arose and went out from that building so happy, that they did not know whether they were on earth or had already gone to heaven." The historian says that the result of that was that in twenty short years, those Spirit-filled Moravians did more for world missions than all the church put together had done in 200 years. They made missionaries out of them. In Hurenhut, they went up, had a prayer chamber and divided it into four-hour segments, so that they kept prayer going twenty-four hours a day for one hundred years. "What happened?" I will tell you what happened. John Wesley was crossing the ocean from the United States to England, when they came into a storm and even the sailors got scared. There was one little group that did not get scared. They huddled together and sang hymns with shining faces. They were the Moravians. And John Wesley said to them, "Why aren't you praying? Why are you so happy?"

They said, "If the Lord wills to have us all drowned, sudden death will be sudden glory."

This dignified Anglican did not know what to make of that, but it went very deep. He went over and found his brother Charles had already been converted. He went to Peter Bowler, the Moravian and said, "Brother Peter, I don't have what you have and I don't have what my brother Charles has. What will I do?"

"Well," he said, "it is by grace, brother, its all by grace."

"Well," Wesley said, "I don't have the grace. What should I do, quit preaching?"

"No," he said, "preach grace because it's in the Bible till you get it, and then after you get it, preach it because you have it."

You all know the story of Aldersgate Street, when John Wesley felt his heart strangely warmed. It is too much known about to mention. Do you know, that wasn't the end of it? Not only did Methodism encircle the globe; the Salvation Army was born out of that. That same Pentecostal outpouring in 1727 spilled over, and the Salvation Army was born out of that as well as the Christian and Missionary Alliance.

Out of the direct descent from the Pentecost that came to the German Christians, back there when the Holy Spirit came on them, bestowed a sense of the loving nearness of Jesus and made them so happy they did not know whether they were on earth or had gone to heaven. They were good, well-behaved Germans but the Holy Ghost came where He ought to be, inside of them. He made Jesus so real that they were so happy they could hardly stay alive.

That is what we need here. We need this.

Oh, may God grant it. Do you want God to do that for us? Do you want God to do that for me, for us? I do. That is the difference the Holy Spirit makes.

CHAPTER 4

# The Abiding Elements
# of Pentecost

I DO NOT KNOW but what this will be the most controversial
of the messages, although my purpose is not to be controversial
but helpful. However, I find you cannot please everybody. Some
say you go too far, and some say you do not go far enough.
Very few are ready to pat your head and say, "I think you
about hit it." Mostly, we are either too far or not far enough.
Because you cannot please everybody, I compromise by trying
to please nobody. But trying to get the truth out and trust that
the Spirit of God will apply it, and that the hungry sheep will
come to the pasture field.

I want to try to discover the abiding elements of Pentecost.
What came and stayed and what came and went? I do
not believe in a repetition of Pentecost, but I believe in a
perpetuation of Pentecost. There is a vast difference there.

This does not contradict anything else I have said. I believe
Pentecost did not come and go, but Pentecost came and stayed.
If we would only get a hold of that. Pentecost came and stayed,
and you and I are living in the midst of it, if we only knew it
and would do something about it.

It is true here as it is true of all spiritual, or at least, all religious experiences, that there are external elements and so were variable. We ought to let the Holy Ghost teach us that God does not care very much for the external. Therefore, the external may be variable.

Then there are the elements that are internal and of the Spirit, and so, they are permanent and they are always about the same.

Then there are incidental elements, which are of relative importance. I would not say they are not important, but I say they are nor critically important.

Then there are fundamental elements that are of vital and eternal importance.

What did happen that day in that upper room there in Jerusalem?

While they were there, suddenly there was a sound in the room "as of" a rushing mighty wind. It did not say that a rushing wind went through there, blowing everything. Nothing like that happened. It said there was a sound "as of" a rushing mighty wind. Did you ever hear a sound that you got the impression that there was a great wind blowing somewhere? That is in nature. That is what it means. It means it was like a rushing mighty wind, the sound of it.

While they were wondering what it was, suddenly there appeared a great cloud of fire, and it divided into little bits and sat on the foreheads of each one present. This fire was the divine Shekinah presence, and it divided and sat upon the forehead of each of them. It says "tongues of fire." You light a candle and you will see it takes the shape of tiny tongue, broad at the bottom and tapering up. That is all it means. It has not any reference whatever to language. It says the fire sat upon their foreheads. Then they began to speak in other languages and the people heard them speak in these languages.

Now, what can't be repeated? What happened there that can never be repeated?

Let me give you some facts.

First, there was the physical presence of all the church together in one place. That could be because there were only about 120 Christians. But it never could be after that, because that day, there were 3,000 more Christians born; and at another time, there were about 5,000 Christians, which made 8,000. I am sure they had no place in Jerusalem that would have seated or even housed 8,000 people. As the gospel went from day to day, the Lord added daily to the church such as should be saved. So finally, it got out of hand and the number of Christians became so large that, no auditorium anywhere would have housed them. No street corner, no open field, no beach, as our Lord sometimes spoke from the boat; no place could they have gotten together.

You hear the words in our time; "ecumenical and ecumenicity." Do not get scared and run when you hear these big words. Preachers like to toss them around because it gives the impression they are very learned. Ecumenical only means universal. It means all over the world; and the ecumenical church just means all the Christians, or as it used to mean, the representative of all Christians. Therefore, an ecumenical council of Christians would be either all the Christians in the world, or at least official representatives of all the Christians in the world. You could have that, I suppose, I do not think it would ever be; but you might envision a gathering of people where there were representatives from all the church from all over the world. Even that would create such a crowd there is not a place in the whole world that would house them.

So the physical presence of all Christians together in one place never was repeated that I know of again. They went on Solomon's Porch, but there were only a small number of them because, when those words were spoken, there were running up in the thousands of Christians and you could not have got thousands on Solomon's Porch. It merely meant that some of them were there.

That was one thing that happened; it never can be repeated again. As far as my knowledge of history goes the sound from heaven was never repeated again. That is, I have not read it anywhere among the Methodists, among the Moravians, among the Presbyterians, or Anglicans. Nowhere have I read of any gathering of Christians where there was sound of a rushing mighty wind.

I have heard that when D. L. Moody called the Christians to gather, he took them out under the pine trees in the eastern part of the United States and kept them there several days and nothing happened.

One day he got up before them and said, "Now the meeting closes tomorrow and we can't go home without being filled with the Holy Ghost." So, he said, "Let's go up and try it once more and wait on God."

They went up among the pine trees and the mighty Holy Ghost came down on them. They went back the next morning and took trains in all directions, and historians record that wherever they went they went, like Samson's foxes going through the fields setting fires everyplace they went. The Holy Ghost had come, but He had not come with the sound of a wind. So that was not repeated.

Then, I do not read anywhere in Christian history where there was the appearance of a great body of fire. You can get some Christians who are just a little bit off beam to say anything. I am talking about trustworthy and reputable Christians who would not overstate things. I do not know any place where there was a great body of fire dividing on the foreheads of the people.

I do not read that anywhere else, at any other time, everybody present began to speak in a language that everybody else could understand without an interpreter. Yet, that is exactly what happened here.

I do not read any place where without interpreters, seventeen different people could hear these people speak and all know what they were talking about.

So, I say, those are elements, which obviously never were repeated, because in every instance they were external.

Now, right here some of you will not like that. But then, I am going to tell the truth and trust God and hope for the best.

Here is the logic of it. That if these things were necessary to the Church, and necessary to the perpetuation of whatever took place there at Pentecost that was basic and fundamental; and then if it was necessary to the Church's life and it was never repeated, then the Church must have ceased to exist the day she was born. Or, at least ceased to exist the day that they died who were present there, about onehundred-twenty.

So, obviously these external things were not the basic things. They were there and were present, but they were external; they were incidental, they were elements that belonged to that particular historic scene and there something was born.

Something came to past. Something was given. A deposit was made. Something happened. And what happened was internal, heavenly, permanent and lasting.

Now what was it that happened that did not pass away? Did not pass away with the sound of the wind. Did not pass away with the sight of fire on the forehead. Did not pass away with the seventeen languages being spoken all at one time. Or being understood at least by seventeen people of seventeen languages. What didn't pass away? What is the eternal and abiding element in Pentecost?

In order to discover it, of course, we have to go and find out what was promised. "And He shall send you another Comforter," said Jesus, "and He shall take the things of mine and show them unto you." Somebody was coming that should make Jesus Christ real.

Then He said, "He will convict the world, the presence of the Holy Ghost in showing Christians Christ and showing sinners their sin." Then He said, "Tarry in the city of Jerusalem until ye be endued with power from on high."

Do you know what happened when He came? Here is what happened. Peter leaped to his feet and shouted, "But Peter, standing up with the eleven, lifted up his voice, and said unto them, Ye men of Judaea, and all ye that dwell at Jerusalem, be this known unto you, and hearken to my words: For these are not drunken, as ye suppose, seeing it is but the third hour of the day. But this is that which was spoken by the prophet Joel; And it shall come to pass in the last days, saith God, I will pour out of my Spirit upon all flesh: and your sons and your daughters shall prophesy, and your young men shall see visions, and your old men shall dream dreams: And on my servants and on my handmaidens I will pour out in those days of my Spirit; and they shall prophesy" (Acts 2:14-18).

As I tried to explain, power means ability to do. That is all it means. Because it is a Greek word from which our English word dynamite comes, some of our brethren try to make out that the Holy Ghost is dynamite. Forgetting that they got the thing upside down. Dynamite was named after that Greek word, and the Holy Ghost and the power of God were not named after dynamite. We ought to remember that. Dynamite was discovered only less than twohundred years ago, but this Greek word goes back to the time of Christ. It means ability to do, that is all. Just ability to do.

One man picks up a violin and he gets nothing out of it but unconscionable squeaks and impossible raucous sounds. He does not have the ability to do. Another man picks up the violin and he is soon playing beautiful, rich melodies. One man sets into the prize ring and he cannot even lift his hands, and the other fellow walks in and he has power to do. Soon the fellow who cannot lift his hand is sleeping peacefully on the floor. The man who has ability to do. One businessman cannot run a peanut stand; he would go bankrupt if he tried even to sell peanuts down on the corner. He has not the ability to do.

One man can step up, open his mouth, and a song will come out. I can step up and no song comes out. Nothing anybody wants to hear.

Ability to do, is what the word means, actually. A dynamic ability to be able to do what you go to do. And ye shall receive ability to do, it will come on you. If you are a soul-winner, you will have the ability to win souls. If you are a preacher, He will give you ability to make the Word plain. Whatever you do in the name of God, He gives you the ability to do.

And He gives you the ability to be victorious in your life, to live right, to behold Jesus and to live with heaven in view. It is ability to do.

Those vital, essential and eternal things took place, came, and stayed. The wind, the fire and the appearance of tongues have never been repeated as far as I know. And all the Christians coming together in one place could not be repeated now, because they are scattered all over the world and you could not get them together. But that the Comforter came, and that He filled them and abode in them, and that He came to make Jesus real and to give them inward moral ability to do right, and inward ability to do God's work; that stayed. That is still here and if we do not have it, it is because we have been mistaught. It is because we have been scared out of it. The teachers have scared us out of it. And some Christians have scared us away from the Holy Spirit.

I remember as a young fellow on the farm in Pennsylvania, when a field of corn was planted and they wanted to save the field from the crows, they would shoot a crow and hang him by his feet in the middle of the cornfield. The point was this, this is a good field of corn but you see what happens to crows that come into this cornfield! That was supposed to scare off all the crows for miles around. They were supposed to hold a conference and say, "Look, there's a field of new planted corn, but don't go near it; I saw a dead crow over there."

That is exactly what Satan has done. He has taken some fanatical, weird, wild-eyed Christian that does things that he should not do, and he has hung him up in the middle of God's cornfield. Then he says, "Now, don't you go near that doctrine of the Holy Spirit, because if you do, you will be acting like him."

I will not be frightened out of my heritage. I will not be scared out of my birthright because somebody did not know what to do with it, or found something else that was not a birthright. I want all God has for me.

Let me point out something here. When Christ was born, many external things happened. They were not of ultimate or vital importance. When Christ was born the angels were notified and they came, but He would have been born whether they came or not. When Christ came, kings came from the east, but He was born whether kings came or not. When Christ came, He was born in a manger and there were all sorts of external circumstances. But there was one great vital fact that never has been taken back. He was born. He did come into the world; He became flesh to dwell among us. He did come and take our human nature, and the word was made flesh to redeem mankind on a cross. That did take place and it remains forever.

These external things are not important. The internal things matter. Thousands of people felt the saving power of Christ but had never heard the angels. Thousands who felt His healing touch had never seen the wise men.

This is the eternal meaning of Acts 2. That the Comforter has come; that deity is in our midst; that God has given Himself to us; the liquid essence of deity has been poured out. He called it, "he hath shed forth this which ye now see and hear."

Let me point out something to you here. Unless we have an outpouring of the Holy Spirit, if we continue to go the way we have been going in fundamentalist, evangelical circles just a little while longer, the fundamentalist will all be liberals and most of the liberals will be Unitarians and there won't be very much left but a few empty buildings.

It is my opinion that we need God's children to realize that they have a heritage, of which they have not taken advantage. God has promised us a unique afflatus, a seizure, an invasion from beyond us that is to come to us and take over and to be in us what we could not possibly be by ourselves.

If you were going to try to write some sonnets as good as Shakespeare wrote like, "Shall I compare thee to a summer's day," what would you have to have? I will tell you what you would have to have; you would have to have the spirit of Shakespeare. You would have to have the intellect of Shakespeare enter your personality. If you and I tried to write, "Shall I compare thee to a summer's day," we would never get any further than that. Winter would come before we would get the second line written. Nevertheless, Shakespeare could make it; he knew what to do with words.

Emerson said that he was the man who, above all men who ever lived in the world, could say anything that he wanted to say. And he did say it. Now, how could you write like Shakespeare?

But if you wanted to write like Shakespeare what would you have to have, The intellect of Shakespeare. If you wanted to compose music like Johanna Sebastian Bach, what would you have to have? You would have to have the spirit of Bach. If you wanted to be a statesman like Gladstone or Disraeli, what would you have to have? You would have to have the spirit of those men.

If we are going to reproduce Christ on earth and be Christlike and show forth Christ, what are we going to have? We are going to have to have the Spirit of Christ. If we are going to be the children of God, we are going to have the Spirit of the Father to breathe in our hearts and breathe through us. That is why we must have the Spirit of God. That is why the Church must have the Spirit of Christ, for the Church is called to live above her own ability. She is called to live up so high that no human being can live like that. The humblest Christian listening to me is called to live a life of miracles; a moral and spiritual life of such intensity and purity that no human being can do it.

Only Jesus Christ can do it. Therefore, He wants the Spirit of Christ to come to His people. This afflatus, this seizure, this invasion from above that affects us mentally, morally and spiritually.

If we just stopped all our busyness; got quiet, worshiped God, and waited on Him; we would rise above the carnality of present Christians. This does not make people love you to say this, and it certainly is not chapter two from *How to Win Friends and Influence People*. But it is true nevertheless that the body of Christians is carnal. We are a carnal bunch. The Lord's people ought to be a sanctified, pure, clean people, but we are a carnal crowd. We are carnal in our attitudes, carnal in our tastes and carnal in everything. The conditions are so shockingly irreverent these days.

One of our missionaries in the Congo told about some missionaries from the United States who came over to his mission field and started singing some imitation Negro Spirituals.

These old deacons took this white missionary aside and said, "Teacher, may we have a word with you? Why do you allow a thing like this? We gave up that junk when we left the jungle and came to Jesus Christ and got some clothes on and were converted. Why do you import from the United States this stuff we gave up and left in the jungle?"

Yet you hear it everywhere you go. Young fellows that ought to be paddled, and here they are with nothing more than silly little jingles, when they should be worshipping.

I say, our Christian services are shockingly irreverent and so degrad our religious face. So largely is our Christian service exhibitionism that unless there is a divine visitation, I do not know where we are going. But wherever we are going, we are going pretty fast. It will never be cured by sermons. It will never be cured until the Church of Christ, you and I, have been suddenly confronted with what one man called the *mysterium tremendum*; the fearful mystery that is God. The *tremendum adjustist*; the fearful majesty that is God. And this is what the Holy Ghost does. He brings this *mysterium tremendum*, this fearful majesty, fearful mystery, this wonderful thing we call God, this wonderful One we call God and presents Him to the human spirit. And when we are confronted with this, out goes our irreverence and out goes our carnality and out goes our degraded religious tastes, and out goes all that. And the soul held speechless trembles inwardly to the furthest fiber of its being. The Holy Ghost bestows upon us a beatitude beyond compare.

Brethren, you will never know more about God then the Spirit teaches you. You will never know any more about Jesus then the Spirit teaches you, because there is only the Spirit to do the teaching. Oh, Holy Ghost, how we have grieved Thee. How we have insulted Thee. How we have rejected Thee. Yet, He is our teacher, and if He does not teach us, we can never know. He is our illuminator, and if He does not turn the light on, we never can see. He is the healer of our deaf ears, and if He does not touch our ears, we can never hear. And yet churches can run for weeks, months and years without ever knowing anything about this or ever having the Spirit of the Living God come at all upon them.

Oh, my heart be still before Him; prostrate inwardly adore Him. This I say is the news I have for you. Deity is present. Pentecost means that Deity came to mankind to give Himself to man that man might breathe Him in as he breathes in the air. That He might fill man.

Dr. A. B. Simpson had an illustration, which I think was about as good as I ever heard. He said to be filled with the fullness of God was like a bottle in the ocean. You take the cork out of the bottle and sink it into the ocean; you got the bottle full of ocean, the bottle is in the ocean, the ocean is in the bottle, the ocean contains the bottle, the bottle contains a little bit of the ocean and so it was with the Christian. We are filled under the fullness of God, but of course, we cannot contain all of God because God contains us.

But, we can have all of God we can contain. And if we only knew it, we could enlarge our vessels. The vessel gets bigger as we go on with God. Deity is among us. If some celebrity were here, the ushers would not know what to do with the people. I tell you, we have a celebrity in our midst. "And it came to pass, suddenly, they were all filled with the Holy Ghost." Deity came down among us and He came down to stay. Not to come and go, but to come and stay. We have eyes, we see not; we have ears and we hear not; we have hearts and we feel not; and we ignore the presence of royalty.

How would the gracious queen of England feel if she were to come to Toronto and not even a policeman on the corner would know she was here? Nobody would know. She would walk down the streets and nobody would even give her a glance. I know, being the gracious little lady that she is, she would probably smile it off, but it would be pretty bad for us, and for the people to know royalty is present and we did not even know it. We have higher than royalty; we have the Lord of lords and King of kings. We have the blessed Holy Ghost present and we are treating Him as though He was not present.

I say, this is terrible. We resist Him; we disobey Him; we quench Him and we compromise with our hearts. We hear a sermon about Him and determine to learn more and do something about it. Then our conviction wears off and soon, we go back to the same old dead level we were in before. We resist the Blessed Comforter. The Blessed Comforter has come to comfort, to teach; for He is the Spirit of Instruction. He has come to bring light, for He is the Spirit of light. He comes to bring purity, for He is the Spirit of Holiness. He comes to bring power, for He is the Spirit of power. He comes to bring these all to our hearts, and He wants you to have this kind of experience.

Years ago, I was up in a little town north of Chicago preaching to a group of Baptist. I told them about Isaiah's vision and these Baptist preachers gathered down front to pray afterward. I went home and got interested in other things. That meeting rather passed into the back of my mind. Two years later two Baptist preachers came to my home and said, "We would like to come in a minute."

They came in. I knew one of them.

He said, "Do you remember when you preached about Isaiah?"

I said, "Yes, I remember."

He said, "I became so thirsty to be filled with the Holy Ghost that I have been a miserable man for two years. I sought God and I sought God, and nothing happened. Here a little while ago, one day in my agony, I was standing in the middle of my living room floor and I looked up at God and said, 'Oh God, You've got to do it.' And I was suddenly, instantaneously and marvelously filled with the Holy Ghost. Now, I am not going out among the Pentecostal people; I am a Baptist and I am going back and preach in the Baptist church. But I just had to stop by and tell you that what you preached two years ago has now happened to me."

Just a Baptist preacher, that is all. God will do that for people and He does not ask you your denominational background. He does not ask whether you are Arminian or Calvinist or what you are. He doesn't ask anything except, are you willing to obey. Are you willing to listen? Are you willing to stop disobeying? Are you willing to stop quenching the Spirit, resisting the Spirit, and throw up your hands and say, "I believe deity is present," and breathe in the Holy Ghost? Let Him come in and fill your life.

I only gave you one illustration but I could give you many more. A young man walked right down here the other night and shook my hand. I recognized him just a little bit, not too much. I went down and he began to talk to me.

"Do you remember when you preached to me so many years ago in Chicago?"

Then I said, "Now I do remember."

He said, "Do you remember what I wanted? I wanted to be filled with the Spirit. I left there and I am here to tell you that it happened to me." The evidence was all over his face of what he was talking about. He was not giving a testimony that someone else had given him.

Now, that is it. Not as dramatic and colorful as you are taught that things ought to be, I suppose. But here we have it. The Holy Ghost came and He is still here. All He wants is for us to yield, obey, open our hearts, He rushes in and our lives are transformed and changed.

CHAPTER 5

# The Dove of Noah's Ark

"BUT THE DOVE FOUND NO REST for the sole of her foot, and she returned unto him into the ark, for the waters were on the face of the whole earth: then he put forth his hand, and took her, and pulled her in unto him into the ark" (Genesis 8:9).

This is an illustration rather than a type and I believe the Holy Spirit put it here for that purpose. I do not wish to enter this strange and beautiful region of the Genesis world, for the landscape is as mysterious as it is lovely, but its scenes are sketchy and fragmentary, and I leave it for somebody else. I want to use this picture of the dove to illustrate why the Holy Spirit has not filled this church.

First, we notice the world as God saw and judged it before the flood. God searched into the hearts of men and He saw that humanity was corrupt and wicked, filled with evil thoughts and imaginations continually. In addition, God saw the ways of man; that they were corrupt, violent and engrossed with immorality, even amid their corruption and violence. The result of what God saw among men was grief to God's own heart. As I said before, only love can grieve. You cannot grieve unless you love and God loved the man whom He had made. The degenerate and corrupt race that descended from Him and His love caused Him to grieve, and it filled Him with anxious care.

Sometimes, in the world of medicine, the kindest thing a physician or surgeon can do is amputate an infected leg and remove that which otherwise would kill the patient. However shocking it may be and however terrible the news might be to the patient, the best news for him is amputation; otherwise it would be death.

Therefore, the dear God who loved mankind looked upon man and saw that moral corruption had gotten such a hold on man, and had gone into the entire bloodstream infecting all the tissues and cells. He knew humanity would die unless He sent a kindly judgment to destroy it and save a few and start over; that the race might not perish, borne down by the spongy corrupt weight of its own sins.

Therefore, God sent a judgment on the earth, and the waters covered the earth as they had formerly covered the sea. And after the passing of a great many days, a great number of days, one-hundred-fifty days, the ark still floated there with eight persons aboard and with two of the animals, birds and all the creatures that would drown, so they did not die. Noah did not take fish nor aquatic animals because they could live in the water, but the ark took all that which would die by the waters of the flood. There they were in the ark, and of course, after the passing of so many days, it had long passed the flood stage where people and things were simply dead. Corruption had already started to set in and when they settled upon Ararat, Noah opened the ark and turned a bird out to see.

The windows of the ark were upward toward heaven and apparently, there were no portholes out, so Noah could not look down. Noah decided to find out from the bird whether there was dry ground below, whether the waters of judgment had assayed. He opened the window and pushed the raven out and we have a sight the like of which is probably very hard to visualize or understand, but there it is, the sight of a dark bird sailing across the desolation.

Now what was that desolation? What did it amount to; what did it add up to?

It added up to the judgment of God; because the angry displeasure of God was on the world and the waters of the judgment, the boiling silt and the floating corpses and all dead things and bits of flotsam and jetsam were there upon the waters. They were a mark of the judgment of God upon the world. The dark bird sailed across the desolation and his dark heart felt at home there for he was a flesh eater and felt at home among the corpses. As that raven sailed away from the warm lighted ark, and from the presence of Noah, he croaked with delight. Out there swollen with internal gases until their hides were as tight as a drum and then wetted with the waters of the flood, these floating things, cattle and all creatures, corpses, human corpses floating there in the waters was a delight to the appetite of the raven. To everything and everybody else, it would have been a repulsive and horrible sight, but the raven was built for it. Something in his dark heart loved it because he lived on it. So, he immediately sailed down, lighted on a likely corpse, and began to tear with his great claws and with his huge beak great hunks of half-rotten flesh. He tore away, ate until he was gorged and sleepy with overeating and then fastened his claws down into the floating things. Happy and restful he went to sleep croaking a good night word to the happiness he found his heart wanted.

Corruption, desolation, silt, flotsam, rotten flesh and dead things fitted his disposition and his temperament; so he fed on the floating death. This is not a type but a brilliant illustration of how things are in the world today.

When man sinned, he deserted God and went out from the place that had been Eden, the garden eastward in Eden, and began to propagate himself. Man had the judgment of God upon him. "But of the tree of the knowledge of good and evil, thou shalt not eat of it: for in the day that thou eatest thereof thou shalt surely die" (Genesis 2:17 KJV).

"And as it is appointed unto men once to die, but after this the judgment:" (Hebrews 9:27 KJV), says God. He is displeased with every man, and unless we repent, we shall all perish and all the nations of the world shall be turned into hell. God is displeased with the nations of the world. He is displeased not only with the east; He is displeased with the west. He sent His judgment not only upon the Iron Curtain countries, but He sends His judgment upon the so-called free nations of the world. So that the great judgment of God is upon humanity, all stock of humanity; red and yellow, black and white, educated and uneducated, cultured and uncultured, cavemen and learned men around the world.

Yet because man has that thing called sin, it doesn't seem to bother people at all because they are just as the raven was, at home in the desolation. His dark heart had an affinity for the judgment and desolation, so it is that men find themselves at home in a world under the judgment of God. The only one good Man that ever came to the world could only manage to stay alive thirty-three years, and then they took Him out and nailed Him on a cross. The better men are, the worse they are despised by those who love the desolation and the darkness that is the sin of the world. Just as the raven never came back to the ark, but lived out there in the desolation, so men have built their civilization upon the floating death you find everywhere.

We like to think otherwise. We are proud of our culture and proud of our bridges, our roads, our buildings and all the things we can do. But God looks on the heart and God says the world is filled with violence. It is filled with violence and corruption and iniquity just as it was then, but the woeful thing is we accept it as such instead of being horrified by it.

We accept it, excuse it, and write books to call it something else.

I think for instance the sodomy of homosexuality that brought the fire of God down on Sodom and Gomorrah. I have seen and read books written to excuse this and to say it is quiet the proper thing. If a man is born with the yen for another man instead of a woman, he is natural and ought not to be criticized. He is living his own nature and we ought not to call it something bad, but it is just his way of living. Learned professors rise, rattle their degrees, stand up and argue in favor of sodomy and every other vice under the sun.

The judgment of God is upon the world. Noah sends out the raven, and the raven never comes back because it is pleased with what it sees.

Noah then sends out the dove. Noah put the dove upon his wrist, and she took off and whirled and banked and turned and banked. Soon he heard the whirl of the wings again; he put out his wrist, she hopped on his wrist and he pulled her back in. She had something in her that could not stand corruption. She could not stand filth. She could not stand bloated corpses. She could not stand what the raven loved, because she had in her not the dark heart of the raven, but she had in her the heart of the dove. It was not for nothing when the Holy Ghost came down upon Jesus; He came in the form of a dove, the pink feet and the round bright eyes of the dove. Ah, those pink feet will never land on anything dirty; those pink feet will never land on anything filthy, and those round bright eyes will never look with love upon anything that is filthy. The dove is a type and picture of the Holy Ghost; harmless, pure, meek, sensitive and loving, and so she came back. She could not stand it. The judgment of God was everywhere, and the silt and the filth and the flotsam was too much for a dove's heart; so she came back and asked to get in the best she could, fluttering against the edge of the window. So Noah pulled her in and kept her there for a while.

Now why did Jesus say, when He spoke of the Holy Spirit say, "Whom the world cannot receive, because it seeth Him not, neither knoweth Him."? There is one thing absolutely that Christians ought to get in their minds, it is that the world knows nothing about the Holy Ghost. The world knows nothing about the Spirit. The world knows about good men. The world appreciates a good man if he gives to colleges and hospitals, runs the clinic to take care of lepers. They will write books about him, and celebrate him. The world knows about good men, but the world has absolutely no affinity for the Holy Spirit, because even good men are under the judgment of God. The best that we have in the world, our universities, our oratorical societies, the best we have apart from the new birth, apart from the presence of God in the life of a man, is only corruption and the wrath of God is upon it.

The world cannot receive it and I think that the most awful, the most terrifying thing that the sensitive Christian heart can hear is the whirling of the wings of God. God wants to come down. He wants to get into our Houses of Parliament. He wants to get into our Congresses and Senates. He wants to get into our United Nations. He wants to get into our groups that play baseball and hockey. God wants to get in, but He cannot get in because the judgment, His wrath, is upon men. His fury is upon the corrupt, violent and vicious world, so the Holy Spirit is restless and He cannot come down. He would come down, for He loves humanity. He loves the blackest sinner in the entire world that might be you or me, because sin is of the heart as well as the body.

Now it would be something else again if all I had to say were that the world could not receive the Holy Spirit. But that which gives me the most concern is that, the Holy Ghost cannot even light upon Christians. Now, every Christian has a measure of the Holy Spirit, let us get that straight. Except a man has the Holy Spirit, he is none of His and when the Holy Spirit converts a man and regenerates a man there is a deposit of the Holy Spirit in the life of that man. That is one thing.

I want you to know my theology is quite sound indeed. I am trying to get through to you a truth I want you to hear, and it is that the Holy Spirit is in some measure resident in the breasts of everybody that is converted, otherwise they would not be converted. The Holy Spirit does not stand outside of a man and regenerate him. He comes in to regenerate him. That is one thing and we are glad and grateful for that.

That is one thing, but there is quite another thing for the Holy Spirit to come down with His wings outspread, uninhibited, free and pleased, to fill lives, to fill churches, and to fill denominations. That is quite another thing. That some measure of the Holy Spirit is in the breast of every man is good and right and real, but that the Holy Spirit wants to come down as the dove wanted to land on the earth on dry ground and could find no place for the sole of her foot, that is also true.

Now the Spirit seeks among us a resting place for His feet and we have called these lightings down. These comings down, we often have called them revivals, and we are languishing for the lighting down of the Spirit. But the simple truth is, unless we have a lighting down upon evangelicalism, upon fundamentalism, upon such churches as our lives churches, unless we have a lighting down, unless the Dove of God can come down with His wings outspread and make Himself known and felt among us, that which is fundamentalism today will in twenty-five years be liberalism. You can be as certain of that. And liberalism will be universalism because this vile world is not a friend of grace to lead us on to God. We are going the other direction.

Have you thought about it my brother? Or are you simply running around being entertained? We must face judgment one of these days. We are going to stand before the Man whose eyes are like fire and out of whose mouth there comes a sharp two-edged sword. We are going to have to talk to Him about deeds done in the body. We are going to have to face what is called the Judgment Seat of Christ and be judged for the deeds done in the body. We are going to have to show Him that we have been serious about all of this; that we were not out to be entertained, but we were out that we might be holy. The Spirit is seeking rest for the sole of His foot. He is seeking it, and yet I hear the fluttering of holy wings and I hear the mourning sound of Him who is grieved and quenched. I see Him looking about for signs of repentance, for signs of sorrow of heart and the lifting of the judgment of God from the church.

When God judges the world it will be terror and fire, but now God wants to judge the church. He wants to judge you and me, His children. He wants to begin at the house of the Lord and He wants to begin to judge us. In the absence of the full power of the Holy Ghost is perpetual condemnation. Now what are the marks of Gods displeasure upon His people? What are the marks of them?

Let me name a few of them for you. Plain sins which nobody can deny; sins of act and habit, sins of selfishness such as reveling in wealth while the world starves, living like kings while millions perish, sins of the heart such as lust. You know you can be a Christian, or at least you can belong to a good church, and still have lust in your heart. You can belong to a good church and still has spite in your heart. Because you go to the pastor, elders or deacons, whoever takes them in in your church, and they cannot look in your heart and know whether you have lust in there or not. We have all cultivated the religious grin. We all manage to look pious when the occasion comes up, so when we apply for membership. We smile piously and they say he is a good young man. But in his heart there is lust, and God hates it and the dove will not come down. He cannot look in a woman's heart and see that she is spiteful there because the woman across the street has a longer car than she has, or a fur coat that costs more. She cannot see resentment that is in the hearts of people and laying there.

There are churches where deacons and elders sit on the same board for years with unconfessed resentment in their hearts. Resentment in the heart of man is just as bad as adultery, and resentment and spite in the heart of the woman is just as bad as the world.

We have this kind of evil thing in our heart; resentment. I have met people that just lived with resentment. You know friends, I just will not stay mad at anybody. I refuse, absolutely. I come from a fiery, nervous English strain. My father's temper was like the trigger on an atom bomb, and he could blow up. I have seen him take a shovel and beat a wheelbarrow in anger. Just beat a wheelbarrow. I got it but I will not stay sour at anybody; I refuse to do it. I refuse to have resentment and ill-will and unforgiving spirit eat at my vitals. Forgive the person for God-sake, forgive him sister. He did not know any better anyhow. Even if he did, he's sorry now; forgive the fellow, and you will feel better inside.

Yet we have it: spite, jealousy, envy and pride. Pride of person and pride of creed and pride of possession, and pride of race and pride of accomplishment.

Then there is coldness of heart toward the Godhead. We sing about God and we pray, but it lacks warmth. And we worship, but coldly and stiffly toward the languishing church. Back in Israel the man of God warned the Jews. He said, "Woe to them that are at ease in Zion, and trust in the mountain of Samaria, which are named chief of the nations, to whom the house of Israel came!" (Amos 6:1). They stretch themselves on beds of ivory and make instruments of music like David, but they are not grieved for the judgment of Israel, and that is where we are.

We are fundamental; sure we are. Carry our Schofield Bibles, sure, we do. We are evangelicals, but the church is languishing and we do not care. At least we do not care very much.

Then there is the poor, sick world out there. I for my part, I do not want to be happy while the world perishes. Nobody loves the world quite enough. The man who loved the world enough to die for it, died for it. And the man who loved Israel enough to want to perish for Israel cried out, "For I could wish that myself were accursed from Christ for my brethren, my kinsmen according to the flesh" (Romans 9:3). That was Paul.

We do not seem to have it much these days. Much of our Christianity is social instead of spiritual. We should be a spiritual body with social overtones. Instead of that, most of our churches are social bodies with spiritual overtones. The heart of the church always ought to be Christ and the Holy Spirit. The heart of the church always ought to be heaven, and God, and righteousness; and they that love the Lord spoke often, one to another, and what they spoke about was spiritual things.

I have met men you could not talk to about anything but God. I have met saints like that, who are so interested in the things of God that nothing else mattered. Ah, my brother and sister, the Holy Spirit loves people like that. He loves that kind of spirit; and He is quick to come, to fill, and to take charge. He wants to do that for us.

Now I close with this story. A man was on a train once. I do not remember where I was traveling from, but he got on and he sat down with me. I knew the man was a missionary from India. He seemed very tender and broken, and he said, "I'd like to ask you something Mr. Tozer. I'm troubled and I'm bothered, and I'd like to ask you something."

I said I am so used to it, just another one I thought.

He said, "This is my problem. A number of years back a strange thing happened on our mission compound in India. We had been having blessing; people were blessed and everything was going all right. But, the missionaries got together for a little conference with some national Christians and we were all sitting around together. A Presbyterian preacher, a missionary, got up to preach to us. He preached, and he sat down. And, Mr. Tozer, I will never be able to describe what happened and I don't know why it happened, but suddenly there came down on that assembly something like a wave of love and light and it broke us up completely. One missionary ran to another one and said forgive me, forgive me. And another ran to another, and they wept and hugged each other. Now, this has resulted in something strange. My home has been completely transformed."

"Now, my wife and I were getting along perfectly well, a normal Christian home, but oh the difference since that time; home is heaven now."

But he said, "Now, that doesn't bother me. Here's what bothered me. Since that time, I am so tender and I weep so easily that it bothers me. When I get up to preach, I am just as likely as not to break down and cry. I was never that way before."

"But," he said, "since the coming down that day, that sudden wonderful visitation, in India, I just cry so easily, my heart is tender. I get up to speak and there it goes again."

He said, "Coming across on this ship I had this experience. They asked me to take chapel on shipboard one morning and I did. They told me there were some Communists who would be present in the service. I took my text; and there it came again, the memory and all the glory came down on me and I just begin to cry, and I couldn't finish my sermon."

I said to him when he finished, "What did the Communist think of it; did they make fun of you?"

"Oh, no," he said. "They were very reverent about it."

Now I am not saying anything good about a Communist; I can't. At least in this case the Holy Ghost shut the mouths of the Communist. And then I said to my friend, "Bert, you've asked me for advice; how can you overcome your tender heart?" I said, "For God's sake brother, don't try it."

We have so many dry preachers, and we have so many men who could not shed a tear. I told him, "If you can keep the tears of God on you and keep your heart tender, keep it brother. You've got a treasure I'd never give up."

But you know how he got that way? The coming down, the lighting down. Now I do not think that Presbyterian preacher had anything to do with it, he might have you know. God could have used him; but they got right with each other, they got cleaned up, they got trouble out of their hearts, and they got their sins put away. Even missionaries got their sins put away, and when there was no more evidence of the displeasure of Almighty God, the Holy Ghost came down.

## CHAPTER 6

# How to Be Filled
# with the Spirit

I BELIEVE IN COMPLETE REALISM; salted, down to earth realism. Not everybody listening to me is going to be filled with the Spirit. But some are and some do, and I thank God. I wouldn't be able to tell you what percentage; but I will be able to tell you that every once in awhile, somebody comes to me with a shining face and says "well it happened, God did it." And from that time on their lives are transformed; they are changed people. Now, unless you are convinced about this, I recommend that you do not do anything yet. I would not want people to come and kneel down and ask God to fill them when they were not prepared. That discourages many people and confuses them. They go away and will not come back and say, "There is no use for me," and they get discouraged.

I would like to have you meditate on the scriptures, read the Word, and see for yourself what God the Lord has spoken. That is first. Before you can be filled with the Spirit, you must be sure that you can be.

Second, you must be sure that you desire to be. But you say, "Doesn't everybody desire to be filled?" And the answer is no. I suppose a lot more people desire to be full, but not many desire to be filled.

Some would like to challenge me on this. I want to be responsible for what I say and I declare that before you can be filled with the Spirit, you must have desire; and some people do not desire.

For example, are you sure you want to be possessed by a Spirit? There are two kinds of spirit possessions: evil spirit possession, where a spirit takes over a human personality as in the days of Jesus and makes them filthy, dumb or evil. Jesus used to cast such spirits out. They were spirits and they possessed these persons.

The Holy Spirit also wants to possess us Christians. This Spirit is like Jesus. Do you want to be possessed by a Spirit that is like Jesus? A Spirit pure, gentle, sane, wise and loving; for that is exactly what He is like. The Holy Spirit is pure, for He is the Holy Spirit. He is wise, for He is the Spirit of Wisdom. He is true, for He is the Spirit of Truth. He is like Jesus, for He is the Spirit of Christ. He is like the Father, for He is the Spirit of the Father. This Spirit wants to be Lord of your life, and He wants to possess you so that you no longer are in command of the little vessel in which you sail. You are a passenger on board or one of the crew, but you are definitely not in charge. Somebody else is in charge of the vessel.

Unfortunately, we do not want it to be that way because we were born of Adam's corrupted flesh, and we want to boss our own lives. I ask you; are you sure you want to be possessed by the blessed Spirit of the Father and the Son? Now, do you want your personality to be taken over by someone who is like this? He will expect obedience to the written Word. We would like to be able to be filled with the Spirit, or full of the Spirit, and then more or less do as we please. But the Holy Spirit who inspired the Scriptures will expect obedience to the Scriptures. And if we do not obey the Scriptures, we will quench Him. He will have obedience and people do not want to obey the Lord.

Every believer is as full of the Spirit as we actually want to be. This sounds like a shocking thing, but it is true. Everybody is as full as they want to be. Everybody has as much of God as he desires to have. The average Christian does not always have as much as he prays in public he might have, or even in private, because there is a fugitive impulse comes to us. We want the thrill of being full, but we do not want to meet the conditions that we have to meet, so we do not want it badly enough to be filled.

Say that you wanted a Cadillac. Some of you have them and some of you want them, but here is Brother Jones; for instance, and he would love to have a Cadillac, but he is not going to buy one and I will tell you why. He does not want one badly enough to pay for it. He wants it, but he does not want it badly enough to meet the terms. Therefore, he goes out and drives his Chevy and that is the way with the Christian. We want to be full, but we do not want to be full badly enough; so we will settle for something less.

We say, "Lord, we'd like to be full. It certainly would be wonderful but we don't want it enough to lay down that kind of money." We do not want to pay the price; we do not want to meet the cost.

The Holy Spirit will expect obedience and will not tolerate self-sins. Self sins, what are they?

Well there is self-love. The church is full of self-love now. In fact, we cultivate it and go to school to learn how to put on and show off. God the Holy Ghost will never allow that. He might allow some Christians to be like that, but He will never allow you to be like that. He will never allow a Spirit-filled Christian to be like that. He is the Spirit that brings humility to the heart; and that humility will be there, or He will be quenched and grieved and He will not fill.

Then there is self-confidence. We are positive we can do things and the Holy Spirit wants to destroy your self-confidence.

As a businessmen, you make decisions; you've got your telephones all over your desk, you buy and sell in big amounts, you make decisions and you're proud of the fact that you run that and make these decisions. Then, you go home and run the house. There is one thing you will not run, brother. You will not run your life after the Holy Ghost gets control. You will not run it anymore; the Holy Ghost will run your life. And the reason you are not filled and full now is that you want to run your life the same as you run your business. You will not dictate to the Holy Ghost. That is the trouble with us; we are dictators, we want to run our lives. We are so full of confidence.

Then we are full of self-righteousness.

We lie to God continually. A man will say, "I am a worm." However, if his wife called him a worm there would be trouble at home. He does not believe it; he is lying to God. He gets down and says, "Oh, Lord, there's no good thing in me." But if you called him a liar, his face would turn white and he would demand what you mean. He does not mean it; he is just lying.

He says he is bad, but he does not believe it. The Holy Spirit wants to take all of that out of you, my friend. He wants to take Adam's righteousness out of you and put another kind in.

And there is self-indulgence. The Holy Spirit wants to take all that out. Along with self-love, self-pity and all the self-sins infesting your life. He wants to take them out. Are you sure you want to be treated like that? Are you sure you want to be filled and possessed by that kind of Spirit? If you are not, if you do not desire to be, then of course you cannot be, because God is a gentleman; the Holy Ghost is a gentleman. He will not come in where He is not wanted.

Then, are you sure you want to be controlled and led by a Spirit who will stand in sharp opposition to the world's easy ways?

The church in our day has become so much like the world that you cannot tell the difference any more. There are a few things we do not do: we do not drink, and most Christians now do not smoke. However, outside of that, they do about everything everybody else does along with trimming their income tax. They take their wives out at lunch and write it on the forms that it was a business engagement. Then we smile and think we are getting away with something. Brother, you are just leaking; your spirit is leaking, your soul is leaking. Scriptures say you put it in "bags with holes in it."

The Holy Spirit will not allow crooked deals. He will not allow sharp shavings; you have to be honest to be filled with the Spirit. Do you want to be filled with the Spirit bad enough so you can stand against the easy ways of the world, live the life of a Christian, the hard life of a Christian?

The Holy Spirit will not allow you to boast or show-off. He will never allow that.

Every time I have boasted about anybody up until now, they have backslid on me. God never allowed me to boast about a convert; he has always backslid as far as I have been able to discover. Every time I have boasted about a crowd, they petered out on me. Every time I have boasted about anything, it went to pot and I thank God for it, because God will not allow that. If I was not His child and His Spirit was not trying to control me and was not succeeding in some measure, I would never hear from God on it. As soon as I start to show off a little bit the Lord sets me flat, and that is exactly the way I want to keep it. That is the way you will be, too. The Lord will never let you show off or boast.

He will take the direction of your life away from you altogether; and He will reserve the right to test you and discipline you, and strip away from you many things that you love and are dangerous to you. We want God and all this too.

A philosophy abroad in Christian circles today says, "I've got God and all this too." I find in the New Testament, when people had God they did not have very much else. They had God and they were rich, but they did not have much else and often times they had to get rid of what they had for Christ's sake.

Our fathers lived this way, but in this 20th century Western Civilization, Canada and the United States are like that together on this. We are rich and well-to-do and have too much. We do not know what it is to suffer and our churches have become a middle class church. We do not know what it is to be poor; we do not know what it is to suffer and lose things, but our fathers did. They paid the price and we will not pay the price. We read books on being filled but we will not meet the conditions.

Consequently, we are all as full as we want to be, my brethren. You are as good a man as you want to be. You are not as good a man as you think you want to be, but you are as good a man as you really want to be. Our Lord said, "blessed are they that do hunger and thirst, they shall be filled." And if the hunger and thirst is theirs sufficiently, they shall be filled. If there is a man hungering after God and is not filled, then the Word of God is broken. We are as full as we hunger to be.

Sometimes we would like to be like D.L. Moody. We would love to be like A.B. Simpson, but not bad enough, and the result is of course we just go on our mediocre way.

I said before you can be filled you must be sure you can be, and you must be sure that you desire to be and you must be sure that you need to be. Why are we interested in this whole subject at all? Can't you get along all right the way you have been? You received Jesus, you said, and were converted and your sins were forgiven. You took a course in the New Testament somewhere and you know you have eternal life and no man can pluck you out of God's hands. In the meantime, you are having a wonderful time going to heaven.

Isn't that enough? Why talk about all this; why do I preach it and why do you come to hear it? Are you sure you can't get along all right the way you are? Or do you feel you just cannot go on, resist discouragement and obey the scriptures, understand the truth and bring forth fruit and live in victory without a greater measure of the Holy Spirit than you know now.

If you have not reached that place then I do not know that there is much I can do. I do not think there is anything anyone can do. I wish I could take the top of the heads of every one and pour the holy oil of God down, but I cannot. I can only do what John the Baptist did when he pointed to Jesus and said, "Behold the Lamb of God that takes away the sin of the world," then he faded out of the picture and after that, everyone was on his own. You had to go to the Lord Jesus Christ and receive help from Christ on your own. No man can fill me and no man can fill you. We can pray for each other, but I cannot fill you and you cannot fill me.

This desire must become all absorbing. I want you to hear this; that the desire to be filled must become all-absorbing in your life. If there is anything bigger in your life than your desire to be a Spirit-filled Christian, then you will never be a Spirit-filled Christian until that is cured. Never. If there is anything bigger in your life than your longing after God, then you will never be a Spirit-filled Christian.

Here is a young couple coming to the altar to be married. As the young woman walks down the aisle to meet her husband-to-be and take the vows of marriage. If she should suddenly discover something bigger in his life than she, when they ask the question will you, she would say, "I will not." She wants to know that she is the biggest thing in his life. If there something bigger in your life, your social and human life, anything bigger than that partner, then yours is not going to be a happy life.

If there is anything bigger in your spiritual life than God, anything bigger than your yearning after God, then you will never be filled. I have run into Christians, who have for years wanted to be filled in a vague sort of way. But the reason they are not filled is they have other things they want more. Because they want it more they either get it or try to get it, but they do not get God. God will not come rushing into a human heart unless He knows He is the biggest thing and nobody has a desire bigger. When God knows that, then God relaxes and rests and smiles and pours out this which "ye now see and hear" as Peter put it.

Now is the desire to be filled with the Spirit the all-absorbing thing in your life? If it is not, then I repeat, we will never get anywhere until it is.

Now I will say this again, I am not sure anyone was ever filled with the Spirit without first having a time of disturbance and anxiety. When I say I am not sure, I mean judging by the Old Testament, the New Testament and Christian Biography and personal experience. And from those four or five ways of testing, I conclude that nobody was ever filled with the Spirit without first having a time of disturbance and anxiety. The Lord's people wanted to be happy, like little children. They want the Lord to give them a rattle; they want to cackle and laugh and they want to be happy. They are going to be happy regardless, but the Lord's happy little children very seldom are filled with the Holy Ghost, because God cannot fill them because they are not ready to die to the thing that makes them happy.

God wants His children to be joyful but not the cheap happiness of the flesh; it is the joy of the resurrected Christ. But before He can fill us, there must be a disturbance and an anxiety. Adam has to die.

It is almost humorous in that Old Testament passage when Saul captured Agag, the sheep and the cattle. Finally, along came Samuel, with his eyes blazing and he said, "Where's Agag?"

He knew Agag was a type of the flesh and that Agag would never be subject to the will of God, could not be and he had to get rid of old Agag. Samuel got a sword. My father used to wet his razor and pull a hair out to see if it would work. When he knew it would cut the hair then he knew it was sharp enough. I can imagine Samuel with that sword, and when Agag saw him, he said, "Verily the suffering of death is past, verily the miseries of death are over." But it was not too long before he was hacked to pieces before the Lord. Samuel did it and got rid of him.

He is a figure there, a type, an illustration at least. Well that has to die, that is why I say there has to be disturbance and anxiety and disappointment and emptiness. I suppose that no Christian who has been filled with the Spirit after his conversion, no Christian but lost his joy. I know I did.

I had a lot of joy when I was first converted; real joy. I was a happy Christian, and to be filled with the Spirit God emptied my joy and showed me it was about half carnality and animal spirits. Sometimes he lets people fall flat on their faces, which shocks them because they thought they were better than that. No, you are not better than that; you just found out how bad you were.

Then there is a despair that comes on the heart of people. Despair with self. As long as you imagine you will make it all right, if you do not want to be too religious, you will make it all right. But it will be a mediocre half-dead Christianity. That is what the trouble is with us. But when you reach that place of despair, when nobody can help you; when you've gone to the last person, you've written the last editor, and followed the last evangelist around, and hunted up the last fellow to counsel with him, and when nobody can help you any more you're in a state of inward despair; that's when you should never despair, because you're near the kingdom. That is getting close, getting near the place where God can do something for you.

But there comes that despair with self; that emptying out of you and that inner loneliness. You know it is part of my belief, I think it is from the scriptures, that God wants to get us to a place that if we only had Him we would still be happy. We do not need God and something else. It is God and something else that is the trouble with us; but when we get God and satisfied that we can have God and nothing else, then God gives us himself and lets us have other things too.

Most of us are too social to be lonely. If we feel a little bit lonely we rush to the telephone and call Ms. Yakity and the next thing we know we have used up a half hour and the buns or biscuits have burnt. However, it is talk, talk, talk. We rush about and it is a social fellowship. There comes a place in your Christian life, my friend, when you will arrive at a place where instead of Ms. Yakity being a consolation to you she will be a pest, and she will not be able to help you at all; there will be nothing she can do for you. It is loneliness for God; you are lonely for God and you want God so bad you are miserable. You are getting close then. You are near to the kingdom, and if you will only keep on you will meet God. God will take you in and fill you and He will do it in His own wonderful, blessed way. I would even say there comes darkness.

The old writers talked about the dark night of the soul; a time of emptying, a time when it became dark all around us. We are too carnal to allow our hearts to get dark with longing for God now. We are so determined to be happy that if we cannot be happy by the Holy Ghost, we will drum up a lot of happiness. We are "rock and rollers," and we are going to get happy somehow if we have to beat it up with a tom-tom. All right, you can have that kind of happiness if you want it. But if you don't want it, and you're dissatisfied with it; and you want the joy that comes out of Joseph's new tomb open now forever; you want the joy that comes from the Holy Ghost; a well of water springing up within you forever. Then you'll likely have a loneliness and inner darkness and despair with self, and you'll wonder what happened to you, and you'll say, "Am I backsliding?" No, you are not backsliding; you are going on with God.

Now somebody will accuse me of being a legalist and saying this disturbance and anxiety, disappointment and despair and all that, earns the Spirit of God. No, that does not earn the Holy Ghost. The Holy Spirit is a gift. He is a gift from the Father to His Children. He is a gift from the wounded side of Jesus to His Children. You cannot pay down one red penny for Him. You cannot turn your finger over it; He is a gift 100 percent.

But what this does for you is not earning the Spirit but it breaks up your fallow ground and it empties the vessel. I say you cannot be full unless you are filled. And the trouble with us is that we are full of too many things now. And God cannot empty us until He brings us to that place of anxiety and emptiness and despair with self. Then, when we are emptied of these things, then the blessed Holy Ghost at least has an opportunity to come in.

D. L. Moody used to take a glass of water for an empty glass and fill it and then ask, "How can that be filled, how could I fill that with milk and how could I fill that glass?" The obvious answer is, you got to empty it. Then Moody would pour it out into another vessel as an object lesson.

There must be an emptying and detachment from the interests of life. Most of us are too concerned with life. We are busy making a living so that we can die of gallbladder trouble or have a heart attack. We are busy making a living, dashing about, keeping our sails up, keeping our business up. Now it is all right and if you are right with God; God will bless you and I am sure He will bless your business too. But most of us do not bother too much about that. We expect to do it and we just want the Lord to have the chariot ready when we are ready to die. Therefore, we kill ourselves long before our time and the Lord takes us home to heaven, so we think.

Brethren, is this too rough? Am I demanding too much? I do not think so. I think I am chilly and cold compared to what I ought to be. I am nowhere near what Charles Finney would have been if he were preaching, or John Wesley or any of the other preachers God blessed and honored.

I will give you four texts, on this matter of how to be filled with the Spirit. Of course, up to now, I have given you conditions and those conditions are part of the how. I give you four texts and I want you to take them. An archangel from heaven could not do any better than to give you the scripture and say believe the Word of God.

First, Romans 12:1-2. You know what it is; I beseech you therefore brethren by the mercies of God that you present your body, that is present your vessel. That's first. A vessel that hasn't been presented will not be filled, and a vessel that isn't presented can't be filled. Present your vessel. I think that God wants us to be intelligent. He wants us to come to Him. If you are in a breadline somewhere in the poor European countries where they have to come with their cups for milk and come with their basket for their bread and you stood back there and didn't present your cup you wouldn't get the milk. If you didn't present your basket you wouldn't get the bread, and if you don't present your personality you won't get fullness of the Spirit of God. Present your vessel.

I give you another verse, Luke 11:9-13. It says, "If a son shall ask bread of any of you that is a father, will he give him a stone; or if he shall ask a fish, will give him a serpent; or if he ask an egg, will he offer him a scorpion?" The answer to all those questions is no. So Jesus draws His conclusion; "If ye then be evil, know how to give good gifts unto your children how much more shall your heavenly Father give the Holy Spirit to them that ask Him."

First, you present your vessel and you ask. That is perfectly logical and perfectly clear. One man who does not believe much in being filled has a note on this verse and says he thinks there is only one person who ever took advantage of that. That is what he thinks. Some of God's people all over the world have taken advantage of that. They did not hear that was not for them, so they believed it and they asked and they were filled.

How much more shall the Holy Spirit be given to them that ask God, so you ask.

The next is Acts 5:32, "We are his witnesses of these things and so is also the Holy Ghost whom God hath given to them that obey him." There must be obedience there. Spirit of God will not give a disobedient child His blessing. He will not fill a disobedient child with the Holy Spirit. There must be obedience there. Obedience to the word, obedience to the Spirit, obedience to the risen Lord. You must be an obedient Christian. He gives His Holy Spirit to them that obey Him.

The fourth text is Galatians 3:2, "This only would I ask of you; received ye the Spirit by the works of the law or by the hearing of faith?" And of course, the answer is by the hearing of faith. Are you so foolish then having begun in the Spirit are you now going to be made perfect by the flesh. You are not filled with the Holy Ghost by law keeping; you are filled with the Holy Spirit by faith and obedience to your Lord.

I want to say the most shocking thing yet. This is the thing that gets you in trouble for saying, but I want to say it.

Here is what people do not want to hear, but I will stand by it so help me God because I do not find it in the Old Testament, or in the New Testament, or anywhere in Christian Biography, or in Church History, or in personal testimonies. I never heard of anybody who had ever been filled with the Holy Ghost who did not know it.

Now some people would like to think they are filled and do not know it; one man tried to explain that. He said that now there is such a thing as static electricity. He said you take a hold of a piece of metal and then you take a hold of another piece of metal or touch it and the sparks will fly off your fingers. You were not filling anything, but you had been full all the time and did not know it. Well the Holy Ghost is not electricity and your soul is something else.

That is a bad illustration, because he is violating the Old Testament and the New Testament, Christian Biography, Church History and all the testimonies of the Spirit-filled saints.

Nobody was ever filled with the Holy Ghost who did not know he had been.

Too, nobody in the Old Testament nor the New Testament nor Church History or Biography was ever filled with the Holy Ghost who did not know when they were filled.

Nobody was ever filled who was filled gradually. Ah, that is where we hide; this filling gradually stuff. The devil knows that if he can just say, well we want to be filled gradually. You don't have to worry about it because it's so slow that you can always encourage yourself; well I'm a little fuller today than I was yesterday, or at least I'm fuller this year than I was last year.

Chances are you are not; but there is no place in the Old Testament where it says the Spirit came on him gradually. Did you ever see it? I never did. The Holy Spirit fell upon them; He came upon them. He filled them, but it was an instantaneous act, never a gradual filling. That is the place for carnal preachers and carnal church members to hide. You can tell how, little by little, slowly the sun comes up, and slowly we open like a flower to the sunshine. Beautiful, you know; lovely poetry but nonsense theologically, and nobody ever got anywhere that way.

Personally, I like the word anointing better than baptism. I am not at all sure that theologically we are not baptized into the body of Christ when we are born again. But the word I want to use is anointing. That anointing is not a gradual thing. When they poured oil on a man's head, it was not gradual. When they poured oil on a fellow's head, it was turning the thing over and pouring it out. It ran all over the beard and down on the skirts of his garments. And everybody for a quarter of a mile around knew they had poured oil on him, because it was the oil of frankincense and myrrh and aloes and cassia and smelled up everything around with its beautiful fragrance. It did not happen gradually; it happened instantaneously.

Now there is where people don't want to be talked to. They say get out with that fellow because I'm perfectly willing to be full of the Spirit, but I don't want to go through the experience of being filled with the Spirit. I am perfectly willing to go on, teach my Sunday school class and tithe and give to missions and be good and witness to the girl beside me at the desk but I do not want to be filled. No, we do not want to lose face you know. Adam does not want to lose face. He wants to be blessed and go to heaven and wear a crown and rule over five cities, but he does not ever want to come to the place where the Lord chops him down.

That is why we are where we are brethren. That is why we are the weak people that we are these days. The Lord's people want Jesus to do all the dying, and they want to do all the chuckling. They do not want to know what the cross means.

"Oh Cross that liftest up my head, I dare not ask to fly from thee; I lay in dust life's glory dead, and from the ground there blossoms red, life that shall endlessly be" (George Matheson).

CHAPTER 7

# Walking in Agreement with the Spirit

MOST PEOPLE WOULD LIKE TO HAVE THE POWER and the peace of the Spirit with a lot of other qualities, and gifts and benefits the Holy Spirit may bring. Now the question is: can we afford to walk with the Spirit? And, are we going to walk with Him? And the answer is: we cannot walk with Him until or unless we are in agreement with Him.

Taking it out of the realm of the Spiritual for just a little bit, and thinking about two people, which is what is meant here; "Can two people walk together except they be agreed?"

That takes us back to the old days when men made long journeys on foot. One man said, "I'm going to a certain town." The other one said, "I am too. When are you going?" "I'm going tomorrow."

Then the question, would they go together, or would each one go off by himself. Now if they were going to go walk together as the disciples at Emmaus, there were a few things they are going to have to agree upon.

One is their direction and the other is their destination, of course. "You're going to such a town?" "Yes." "Well I am not." Therefore, they would have to shake hands and depart because two men cannot walk together when one man is going to one city and the other to another. At least they cannot for very long.

Then they would have to agree on which path to take if there were several paths. They would have to agree on the rate of speed. One man said, "I am a very fast walker," and the other man said, "I just clump along; I hardly make it at all." They would say, "Well there's no use for us to walk together, because I am so slow I would bore you." The other man would say, "No, I'm so fast that I would trouble you." So, they would not go together.

Then, they would have to agree they wanted to walk together; did they want to walk together. There are some people that, if I was going to walk from here to Hamilton, I would just as soon walk by myself. I love them all right, and I pray for them, but I do not find them edifying companions. You have to decide whether you want to walk together or not. Whether it is advantageous to both parties concerned. Whether there is incompatibility that might render the trip unpleasant.

For two to walk together voluntarily, they must be one. They must agree on the things that matter if they are going to walk together. Now that bears upon the subject I want to talk about, and you will quickly see how it bares. How to cultivate the Spirit's companionship; how to walk with the Holy Ghost.

Some people are just not ready to hear what I have to say, and of that I am convinced. Some are not willing to give up all to obtain all. They are not willing to turn toward God and walk with Him. They are facing both ways. John Bunyan talked about Mr. Facing Both Ways. A great many Christians, even gospel Christians, are facing two directions at once and they are not willing to go along one way. They want some of the world and some of Christ. They allow the Lord to disturb their way, but they also disturb the Lord's way. And they do not get together on this. And there is no use of us talking about being filled with the Spirit and walking in the Spirit unless we are willing to give up all to obtain all.

Then there are Christians, and a lot of them in our gospel churches, that want Christianity for its insurance value. That is they want the care and protection that God gives them now. They want avoidance of hell at the time of death. They want the guarantee of heaven at last. To get this, they are willing to support the church, and missions, and other religious projects financially. And, who would not be willing to pay his insurance, if he knew it would help him in the hospital if he got sick; or got into an accident, it would pay his widow a lot of money if he died. Who wouldn't be willing to pay and support that kind of insurance? Christianity, to some people, is simply there for its insurance value. They want its protection and what it has to offer and guarantee of heaven at last. Now I say, they are willing to support it, and they are willing to abstain from certain gross or pleasures. I do not think you will have much difficulty getting the average person to quit gambling if he has been a gambler. I don't think you'll have much trouble getting the average man separated from a lot of the fleshly things, because you know there are a lot of sinners that don't do certain sins; there's a lot of sinners.

My father used tobacco, both smoking and chewing for, I guess, fifty years. One day he looked at the stuff and had a sudden revulsion of feeling. He said what a dirty mess that is after-all, and he turned his back on it, and never touched it again, even until he died. He was not converted for many years after that. Between the time he gave it up and the time he was converted, a period of perhaps eight to ten years, he just did not like the stuff anymore.

Not every sinner is dirty, not every sinner is a rascal; not every sinner cheats on his wife; not every sinner refuses to pay his debts. There are honorable men and good men and honest men, who will tell the truth if it hurts, right out in the world, that have no hope of eternal life nor heaven to come, that are not followers of the Lord; they're just decent people. The idea that everybody is a wicked rascal and a scoundrel is all wrong. I have known some of the finest men who are not Christians.

I know a man in Chicago who is so good that everybody wants to make a Christian out of him, but he steadfastly refuses, and says, "I am not a Christian, I am not a Christian. But he is so good that he puts to shame many Christians. He does not claim that he is winning his way to heaven; it is not a question of the old morality that the evangelists talk about. He does not believe in that. He just knows he is lost, but he is also a man of incorruptible character; he is a good man. And of course, many Christians are willing to give up the grosser things and live in a reasonably decent way.

Some people are not ready for this message. Their conception of religion is social and not spiritual. They water down the strong wine of the New Testament until it has no tang in it anymore. They water it down with their easygoing opinion. They are very broad minded, they imagine, but the fact is they are so broad minded, they cannot walk on the narrow way. And many Christians now are more influenced by Hollywood than they are Jerusalem. That is just as sure as you live, that is their spirit; their mood is more like Hollywood than it is Jerusalem. If you were to sit them down in Jerusalem, they would wonder around, even as in the days of Christ, and would not feel at home. Take them out to that nest of iniquity in California, and they would say I wonder who she is. I wonder if she is one of the stars. They would be quite at home there, because their mood, the texture of their mind, has been created for them by twentieth century entertainment and not by the things of God.

Some people would like to be filled with the Spirit for the thrill of it. They want to be thrilled and they would pay almost any price to get the thrill. However, they will not die to themselves, to the world, or to the flesh. Hence, for these, what I have to say now will have no sympathetic meaning whatsoever. You just cannot have any meaning, because they have not come over into the region where God can get to them. Thank God, there are always some. And I do not know who they are. It is impossible for me to know. Among the things God has not done for me is to give me the ability to put my finger on a man and say, thou art the man or thou art not the man. God keeps His mysteries and His secrets from me to some extent, so I cannot tell you who they are. But I know there are some who have said, "Jesus, I my cross have taken all to leave and follow thee." And from somewhere has come a longing, a blessed aspiration; a deep longing, a yearning after God that is so real and so wonderful and so pain filled that they know what I am talking about sympathetically.

You see, there is a difference between knowing doctrine intellectually and knowing it sympathetically. Anybody can learn the catechism and know the doctrine intellectually. And we have Bible Conferences all over the United States and all over Canada, all over England, all over Scotland and Wales and all over the world. Wherever Christianity is heard, we have Bible Conferences, and we take a week to ten days to study the Word. And its good and you can get a hold of the Word of God intellectually. It is quite another thing to let the Word of God reach you sympathetically; that is, your heart goes out sympathetically to the Word of God and it reaches you sympathetically.

I think there are some here like that and maybe more than I think, for I will break down and tell you something. I am not an optimist except in the long-range eschatological sense. If you do not know what eschatological means ask me. I do not know whether I do, but I am thinking now about the long-range future event. I am an optimist in that, but not too much of an optimist when it comes to things of now. I am likely to underrate than overrate. You will find that out now if I stay around here much longer. But maybe there are more people hungry for God than I know. Maybe so, and I sincerely hope so; and if there are and if there is even, one then I want to give this second half of my talk now.

If you are a hungry person and Christ is more to you than an insurance against hell, and Christianity is to you more than an opportunity to mingle socially with good people; If God is real to you and Christ is real, and your heart is longing after God and you want the best God has and your heart is open to the Holy Spirit's incoming, then I want to give you a few thoughts now.

First, the Holy Spirit is a living person. That is, He can be known in increasing degrees of intimacy. This is the second time I have said, this but I want to emphasize it tonight that since the Holy Spirit is a personality, He is never fully known in one encounter. One of the biggest mistakes we can possibly make is to imagine that, by coming to know God in the new birth and receiving the Spirit of adoption whereby we cry Abba Father, we know all we can know about God. And people of our persuasion make the second mistake, which is being filled with the Holy Ghost after conversion.

Some think they know all there is to know about the Holy Spirit. Oh, my friend, you have just started. For God's personality is so infinitely rich and manifold, that it will take a thousand years of close search and intimate communion even to begin to know the outer edges of the glorious nature of God. So that when we talk about communion with God and fellowship with the Holy Spirit, we are talking about that which begins now, but which grows and increases while life lasts. Everything else being equal, if you are a seeker after God. as I hope you are, and you go on in obedience, you will know God much better five years from now than you know Him now.

And if you do not know Him better now than you did five years ago, then you have pretty much wasted five years of your life. You know it is possible to do that. Jacob wasted twenty years of his life and then went back to the altar, had his second experience by the river Jaboc, had his name changed from Jacob to Israel and went on from there. However, twenty years was taken out of his life. And I find Christian people that have wasted their lives. They have been converted to Christ, but they have not gone on to know the Lord increasingly. They have accepted the cold level of things round about them being normal. Well, there is untold loss and failure. This idea that was current a few years ago. People are a little more modest about that now.

I think Mussolini, the Roman Empire and a few other things rather blew up in our faces, and we are not quite as sure of ourselves as we used to be when it comes to prophecy. I used to hear young fellows, you know, who weren't dry behind their ears yet get up and talk about reigning over five cities, how many crowns they were going to wear and all that sort of thing. They were not going to wear any crowns nor reign over any city, but they thought they were. They had it all worked out theologically. But they were not getting on to know God. They were just opening the Word, as they call it, and teaching the Word about five crowns of the Christian and that sort of thing.

Well, they are suffering loss nevertheless; suffering loss because they are bogged down in their teachings and have not gone on to know God for Himself.

So the Holy Spirit is a living person. And as He is a living Person, you can know Him and fellowship with Him; whisper to Him and have His voice whisper back to you in some love text that you know, or some love hymn, and whisper back to you, so that walking with the Spirit can become a habit with you. Something you can do so that you can be in His presence, conscious of His presence, so you will not always have to talk. I think I mentioned before that there are two kinds of friendship. There is the tentative and uncertain kind of friendship that does not allow you to sit down and look at a magazine when you come to their house, or just sit down and snooze. They have to be entertaining you, because they do not know you well enough and you do not know them well enough to relax. Nobody relaxes. You are company; they are entertaining you and somebody must be talking every minute in order for you to know you are welcome.

After you know these people, and you grow in the knowledge of each other and your friendship becomes bigger, sweeter, and broader, you can go to their house or they to yours and not say anything for ten minutes at a time and nobody will think you are mad. Then your friendship has passed by the place where it has to be kept up by chatter. And I believe it is possible to get to a place where we can know God so intimately that we do not always have to be chattering to God. We can pray and inwardly we do pray, but we do not have to all the time.

I remember once riding with a preacher, and we had to make a certain engagement where I was to preach. We were riding along in the rain some years ago, and in those days the cars were not closed up much underneath, and when it splashed, it got water in the points, and the car would stop. This poor fellow was driving, and I was sitting beside him, and it was raining hard. The car would sputter, and he would pray to beat the band: "Oh, God, keep it going, keep it going, God." Then, when it would stop sputtering, he would talk a little; and then it would sputter some more, he would pray a little more, and he was just so worried there; he and God had not had any understanding about that at all. Apparently, they were not closely enough acquainted so they could relax, or at least he could relax. I think God was relaxed about the whole thing, but my preacher friend was not.

It is possible to know Him in increasing intimacy. I want to ask you, do you know God better now than you knew him a year ago? I want to ask you, do you know God more intimately, warmly, than you knew Him a year ago? Are you growing in grace? I do not say has it been an even motion upward, like a flight of a plane, gaining altitude. Because it has been my experience and experience of Bible Christians, and I find the same thing true in Biography, that we do not take off from a ramp, mount straight up toward God and continue to mount. We zigzag up, and zigzag up. But the point is, when the zigs and the zags have been ironed out, are you nearer to God now than you were a year ago? Are you closer to the heart of God now? Allowing for the bumps that you had during the time, allowing for the times of coldness, are you closer now than you were a year ago. If you are not, something is seriously wrong, and you should consider doing something about it no later than tonight.

Now, how can I cultivate that holy fellowship?

I will tell you; be engrossed with Christ. Honor Christ and the Holy Ghost will honor you. You remember that Jesus, on that last day of the feast, lifted up His voice and cried and said "He that believeth on me, as the scripture hath said, out of his belly shall flow rivers of living water. (But this spake he of the Spirit, which they that believe on him should receive: for the Holy Ghost was not yet given; because that Jesus was not yet glorified.)" (John 7:38-39 KJV). The pouring out of the Holy Ghost depended upon and waited upon, the glorification of Jesus Christ the Lord.

When Pentecost was fully come, Peter got up to preach a sermon and reflected back to that same passage and said, "Be it known unto you all, and to all the people of Israel, that by the name of Jesus Christ of Nazareth, whom ye crucified, whom God raised from the dead, even by him doth this man stand here before you whole." (Acts 4:10 KJV)

Always remember that you will know the Spirit more intimately as you make more of Jesus Christ the Lord. For Jesus said the Holy Spirit would take the things of His and show them unto us.

We walk with the Holy Ghost when we walk with Christ. For Christ will always be where He is honored. The Holy

Ghost will always honor the one who honors the Savior Jesus Christ the Lord. Let us honor Him by giving Him His right title. Let us call Him Lord, let us believe He is Lord, let us call Him Christ. Let us believe He is Christ, and let us get away from this cheap Jesus dear kind of stuff that pulls Christianity down to the world of erotica and makes it half-sexy.

Let's get rid of that whole silly business and remember, "God has made this Jesus, whom ye crucified, Lord and Christ; and set Him at His own right hand and put all things under His feet and made Him to be head over all things of the church; and He shall reign from the river to the ends of the earth." This is the Christ we adore and let us be careful to honor Christ; always honor Christ. Honor Him by obedience, honor Him by witness, honor Him by testimony; and as we all honor Christ, then we will fellowship with the Holy Ghost.

Again, to know the Holy Spirit in increasing intimacy of companionship, walk in righteousness. Walk in righteousness, because we might as well face up to it my brethren; God cannot possibly have fellowship with a man or woman that is not living right or not walking right. We have magnified grace all out of proportions to the Bible. Paul says, with weeping, that men had turned the grace of God into lasciviousness, and we have done the same thing now. We are so afraid that we will reflect upon the all sufficiency of grace that we dare tell Christians that we have to live right. But remember, Paul in the Holy Ghost wrote his epistles and in those epistles, he laid down holy inward ethics; moral rules for the inward Christian. Read it in Romans and Corinthians and Ephesians, and Colossians and Galatians, and see whether it does not all add to the same thing. Read the Sermon on the Mount and the other teachings of Jesus, and see if He does not expect His people to be clean and right.

I wrote an editorial for the Alliance Witness, and at the same time, it was printed in London in a magazine, "The Life of Faith." I was rather amused when I discovered they were taking me to task. I was over here having a nice time; over there they were writing hot letters back and forth to each other about me. One fellow said, "Tozer does not distinguish between discipleship and salvation; to be a disciple and to be a Christian." Another responded by saying, "He said you could be a Christian without being a disciple."

Whoever said you could be a Christian without being a disciple? You cannot be a Christian without being a disciple. The idea that I can come to the Lord by grace, and have all my sins forgiven, and have my name written in heaven, have the carpenter go to work on a mansion in my Father's house and at the same time I can raise hell on my way to heaven. I say it is impossible. It is unscriptural, it is not found in the Bible at all. You are not saved by your good works, no never are we saved by our good works, but we are not saved apart from good works. We are saved by faith in Jesus Christ alone, but out of that, springs immediately goodness and righteousness.

Flowers do not bring spring, but you cannot have spring without flowers. It is not the birds that bring the summer, but you have no summer without birds. It is not righteousness that saves me but salvation brings righteousness. The man who is not ready to live right, he is not saved; he will not be saved, and he will be deceived in that great day.

I spent some thirty-one years in a town that is, or was for a good many years, the Mecca of evangelical Christianity. It is pretty hard to preach this there without getting into trouble. But I preached it all right and kept on preaching it; and before I left, I was being heard by everybody. And the very persons who before had held another view were listening to me, and I am preaching it to you now, that we must walk in righteousness. I cannot for the life of me see how it is possible that we can support the doctrine that Christians ought to be good people. Christians ought to be the best people in the world. And I could not believe a man is on his way to heaven when he's performing such deeds as indicate that, logically he ought to be on his way to hell.

So walk in righteousness and see to it that you do. And make your thoughts a clean sanctuary; to God our thoughts are part of us. The Spirit is all seeing and all hearing and all loving and pure, and He cannot endure thoughts of malice. Can you imagine a man with malicious thoughts in his heart having companionship with the loving Holy Ghost? No, it is impossible that he should. Can you imagine a man bloated with egotism knowing the Holy Spirit with anything like intimacy? No, he could not possibly do it.

Can you imagine a man who is a deceiver ever having any fellowship with the Spirit? Never. Can you imagine it? It is folly to believe it my friend. If you have habitually given over to thinking dirty thoughts, you are habitually without the communion of the Holy Ghost, let me tell you that. Keep your mind pure.

This gossip business; God deliver us from it. But its here, we have it to deal with and if we do not deal with it, it will deal with us. I have even found that prayer groups are gossipers. Some sister will get up and say in a high, shocked voice, "Now I would not mention this except I want you to pray." The old hypocrite, that is not it at all. She is just gossiping and she wants to do it publicly. And she says now, "I want you to pray for Mrs. Jones. I looked in the window as I went by and Mr. Jones and Mrs. Jones were arguing, and I'm sure there's a fight in that home." And the old sister would love to have had a bug in there, a microphone, and just heard the whole thing. She would not smoke a cigarette, and she sneers down her holy nose at any woman who would smoke, but she loves a bit of dirty gossip.

Then she says, "I was filled with the Holy Ghost at such and such a Camp Meeting." Well she's never gone on from there. In fact, she has gone back from there, because one of the things the Spirit of God will do for a person is to make them so they don't want to gossip about people. They may be driven; it may be necessary for them to talk about things that are not good and they may have to sometimes if they're on committee's, or they're choosing a teacher or anything else. They may be compelled. I have been many a time compelled to deal frankly with people's characters, but that is one thing. It is quite another thing to love to hear gossip about people.

Make your thoughts a clean sanctuary. Clean out the sanctuary the way old Hezekiah did back there. They had dirtied up that sanctuary, and when Hezekiah took over, he got all his priests together and it took them several days and they carried out all the filth and burned it. Threw it over the bank and got rid of it and went back and sanctified the temple, and then the blessed God came and they had their worship again. Well then, I would also suggest that you seek to know Him in His Word.

Now remember that He inspired the Word and He will be revealed in the Word. I have no place in my sympathies for Christians who neglect the Word, ignore the Word or get any revelations apart from the Word. This is the book, after all, my friends, "Oh Word of God incarnate, Oh wisdom from on high, Oh Word unchanged, unchanging, Oh light of our dark sky." This is the book; and if we know the book, well enough we will have an answer to every problem in the world that touches us. But some people get far off the track. I stay by the Word; I want to preach the Word and love the Word and make the Word everything. Read it much, read it often, brood over it, think over it, meditate over it, meditate on the Word of God day and night. When you wake at night, think of a verse. When you get up in the morning, no matter how you feel, think of a verse and make the Word of God everything.

Because the Holy Ghost wrote the Word, and if you will make a lot of the Word, He will make a lot of you. He will make a lot of the Word and He will make a lot of Himself to you. For it is through the Word that God reveals Himself. This is not a dead book between covers; this is a living book. God wrote it and it is still alive. This book is still alive; it is a living, vibrant book. God is in this book. The Holy Ghost is in this book. And if you want to find Him go into the book. If you want to find the Shepherd, you know where to look, find His sheep and you will find the Shepherd. And if you want to find the Holy Ghost, go where the Holy Ghost inspires in the book itself and you will find Him there. I know it is possible to know doctrine without the Spirit, and I have said that a while ago. It is possible to know the doctrine intellectually, not know it sympathetically, and still not find the Holy Ghost there.

But do not try to cultivate the Spirit without the Word. There is an awful lot of that now. A lot of humanism over-larded with a lot of paganism over-larded again with a bit of esoteric religion, nature, poetry and philosophy of sweet old ladies and all that. Now that will not do friends, it is not enough, it is not enough. I believe in great hymns but all these cute little things that people write when they should have been looking after the baby, and then they get them into print and want me to place them in my Bible and read them. I will not do it. I would rather pass them over, forget them, go to the Word itself.

Then I would say, cultivate the art of recognizing the presence of the Spirit, everyplace, all the time. The Spirit of the Lord fills the world. The blessed Holy Spirit is here and you cannot walk out away from where He is. You cannot hide away from Him; David tried it in 139th Psalm. He said, "I found that I could not do it. I went up into heaven and you were there, if I go down to hell, you are there and if I go to the uttermost parts of the sea, you are there, and if I say darkness hides me I find God shines even in the darkness." He said, "I could not get away from God." If you are interested in Him, you will find Him where you are. The presence all about you.

I would recommend that you find out what it is that has been hindering you. Nobody wants to be asked that question.

But find out what it is that has been hindering your life. You have not progressed; you do not know God as well as you did or at least any better than you did. What is the trouble? Well the Lord's people do many borderline things. Let me give you an example.

A friend of mine who is now in heaven, H.W. were his initials. He used to write me a letter and say, "Dear A.W." and sign it, "H.W." A dead soul, a dear man of God.

He came in one time from a missionary convention where he had been the preacher and he told me this.

"Brother Tozer, we are in desperate need of revival out in a certain section in the Alliance."

And I said, "Is that so. What lead you to that conclusion?"

"Well," he said, "here is an example. We were having our missionary convention throughout the week, and it went along all right until Friday night. Friday night the pastor came to me and said, 'Now tonight, we are going to shorten the meeting a little bit. You'll be on last, and I want you to quit so that we can be out of the building with the lights out by ten minutes of nine.'

"He told me, 'the missionary will talk, and we cannot always tell how long the missionary will go, and there will be singing and some announcements and an offering and then you will preach. I do not care how long you preach, only one thing, remember tonight, we must be out of the building at ten minutes of nine.'

"I said all right, and I got through about a quarter of nine and they sang a verse and prayed and went home. The building was empty ten minutes of nine. Later on, I found out why this pastor was shortening the meeting and rushing us out of the church. Friday night was the night the fights came on television and the pastor could not give up his Friday night fights."

Two bruisers knocking each other's brains out up there, if they ever had any to start with, and he had to see that. It had so hooked him, it had so hooked him that he closed a missionary convention even though Jesus said to "tarry until ye be endued with power from on high, and then go and preach the gospel to every creature." And these missionaries were there, giving up everything to go, but this pastor had to shorten the meeting to see the fights.

In a hotel room in New York City, I set one time with nothing in the wild world to do and I watched a fight. I am not saying it is a deeply sinful thing to do, but in the context, it was deeply sinful and iniquitous for a pastor to be so caught up in a thing that he grieved the Holy Ghost and quenched the Spirit and insulted God.

Now brethren, find out what it is; it may not be that with you. And the rule is, does this hide the face of Jesus a little bit from me? Does this chill my heart a little? Does this take the joy out of my Spirit? Does this make the Word of God a little less sweet? Does this make earth a little more desirable?

If you answer yes to those questions, then you're going to have to do some repenting, and some cleaning up before the blessed Holy Ghost will come to your heart and warm it and refresh it and make it fragrant with His presence. This is how we cultivate the Spirits friendship.

Somebody said, "That kind of living, Mr. Tozer, is narrow and old fashioned, and I would be deprived of so many things." Now is not that just terrible that you would be deprived of a few cheap trinkets if you followed God.

What would you think of a woman who would balk at going down the aisle to marry the man she is supposed to love if she said to him, "listen, at home I've got a big house, my father looks after me; I don't have to work and I just can't give up these comforts to marry anybody." That is exactly what we are telling the Lord. We are saying, "Lord, these are things that I have always enjoyed doing and I am not going to make any changes for Thy sake."

You will never hear any talk back from God, never. As the Welsh preacher said, "God is a gentleman and He always knocks at the door; He has never pushes it open and He never barges in. He waits to be wanted, He waits to be invited and He waits to be loved." And if you would rather have the cheap trinkets of the world than to walk with the King of Glory, you can have it dear friend. You will get no argument from me; you will get none from God.

Remember, He is a Person and can be cultivated just as you cultivate a friend. Remember, you must be engrossed with the Person of Christ for He glorifies Christ. Remember, you must walk in righteousness, for God will not fellowship anyone who deliberately lives in sin. Make your thoughts a clean sanctuary; be clean inside as well as out. Seek to know Him in the Word. Live in the Word so the Holy Ghost can live in you. And cultivate the art of recognizing the presence of the Lord and of the Holy Spirit everywhere, at all times.

Then find out what is hindering you and put it out of your life. Well that is simple enough is not it, nothing fanatical about it. Only I wonder if we are going to pay the price.

# *The Realm of the Spirit*

I WISH ALL CHURCH PEOPLE MIGHT HEAR THIS, that the realm of the Spirit is closed to the intellect. It is not difficult to understand why. You see the spirit is the organ by which we apprehend divine things, and the human spirit is dead because of sin. Therefore, the human intellect is not the organ by which we apprehend divine things.

For instance, if a symphony was being played just now, you do not hear that symphony with your eye, because God did not give you your eye to hear with. He gave you your eye for vision, not hearing. If there were a beautiful sunset, you would not enjoy that with you ear because God did not give you your ear to hear sunsets with. He gave you your ear to hear music and the voices of your friends and the laughter of children and birdsong and all things beautiful and good. He gave your ear to hear all things that can be heard; He gave you your eye to see what can be seen. But He never confuses the two. You do not hear with your eye nor see with your ear.

If I stand up and say the realm of nature, the ear cannot apprehend visible nature. Nobody wonders, nobody jumps up and says, "That man is a mystic." It is just common sense, it is ordinary scientific fact. So, when I say God did not give you your intellect to apprehend Him with, but He gave you another organ altogether, then there is certainly nothing profoundly unclear about it.

Look at this passage. "For my thoughts are not your thoughts, neither are your ways my ways, saith the Lord, for as the heavens are higher than the earth so are my ways higher than your ways and my thoughts than your thoughts."

And 1 Corinthians 2, "But the natural man receiveth not the things of the Spirit of God; for they are foolishness unto him: neither can he know them because they are spiritually discerned."

"The natural man," that is, the man of mind and the intellect, cannot understand nor receive the things of the Spirit of God. They are foolishness to him and he cannot know them because they are spiritually discerned. God gave us spirit to apprehend Him and intellect to apprehend theology. There is a difference.

And in John 16, Jesus said "I have yet many things to say unto you, but ye cannot bear them now, howbeit, when he the Spirit of truth is come, he will guide you into all truth, for he shall not speak of himself, but whatsoever he shall hear that shall he speak and he will show you things to come, he shall glorify me for he shall receive of mine and shall show it unto you."

Now it is perfectly plain that the Spirit of God is the One who reveals God to us.

In 1 Corinthians 2, we have a passage there also that tells us: "Howbeit we speak wisdom among them that are perfect: yet not the wisdom of this world, nor of the princes of this world, that come to nought: but we speak the wisdom of God in a mystery, even the hidden wisdom, which God ordained before the world unto our glory: but as it is written, Eye hath not seen, nor ear heard, neither hath entered into the heart of man, the things which God hath prepared for them that love Him."

Isn't it strange how many times we stop when we should go on, we go on when we should stop. Here is one of the places where people stop; we memorize that verse and put a full stop after the word Him. God hath prepared for them that love Him and then we stop there, but the Bible does not stop there. It has a little conjunction "but" there. It says, "But God hath revealed them unto us by His Spirit. Eye hasn't seen nor ear heard, nor the heart of man understood but God has revealed it by the Spirit." The eye does not apprehend the spiritual things; the ear does not apprehend them and they are not apprehended even by the intellect, but the Spirit reveals them, for the Spirit searches all things, yea the deep things of God. Then He uses an illustration and says, "What man knows the things of a man, save the Spirit of man which is in him."

This is what we call intuition. You know what you are and who you are, and even if you did not know your name and even if you were visited with the disease that takes away your memory, you would still know you are you. You intuit it. You know you are alive, you do not reason that you are alive.

Rene Descartes said, "I think, therefore I am." But that was silly because he knew who he was even before he ever reasoned it; he knew who he was by intuition. Now that is the problem with the church in our day. We forget that there is something you cannot get a hold of with your head. We run around with our heads always trying to lay hold of things with our minds. Now the mind is good. God put it there. He gave you a head and He did not give it to you so your glasses could be on it, or your hat. He gave it to you and He put brains in your head; and the organ we call the intellect has a work to do, but that work is not apprehending divine things. That is of the Holy Ghost.

That is why when a person is truly converted you cannot argue him out of it. While the world stands, he knows he is converted. He intuits it. The Holy Ghost tells him deep within his heart. He does not have to have three or four fellows beat him on the back and stick a marked New Testament under his nose. He knows he is converted by the inworking of the Holy Ghost that intuits it. He knows it. Now he said, "even so the things of God knoweth no man but the Spirit of God." God knows himself and the Holy Ghost knows God, because the Holy Ghost is God and no man can know God except by the Holy Ghost.

To disregard what I am talking about, is to shut out spiritual things entirely from our understanding. Spiritual things are hidden behind a veil according to this, and the son of earth cannot get a hold of them; he comes up against a blank wall. He takes doctrine, texts, proofs, creeds and theology and he lays them up like a wall, but he cannot find a gate and he cannot find any light. He stands in the darkness and all around him is intellectual knowledge of God, but not the personal knowledge of God. There is a difference you know.

It is possible to grow up in a church, learn the catechism and get everything from sprinkling the baby on down to the last rites. After you have done all that, you may not know God at all. Because God is not known by those external things. You are blind, you cannot see because "the things of God knoweth no man but the Spirit of God."

There has been a great blunder in more modern orthodoxy. It is the erroneous assumption that spiritual truths can be intellectually perceived, and there have been far reaching conditions resulting from this. It has shown itself in our preaching, in our praying and in our singing, and in our activity and in our thinking. It is an error to believe that Bible study can remove the veil. When you go to Bible school, you learn theology; New Testament introduction, Old Testament introduction, New Testament synthesis and Old Testament synthesis, and think you have something. You could have something provided you had the divine illumination of the Holy Ghost. However, until you receive that illumination, that inward enlightenment, you do not have anything, because Bible study does not of itself lift the veil and penetrate it.

Let me give you a little motto, before I can understand a Bible text it takes an act of the Holy Spirit equal to the act that inspired the text in the first place.

2 Timothy 3:16 says, "All scripture is given by inspiration of God and is profitable ..."

John 3:27 which says, "A man can receive nothing, except it be given him from heaven."

But we are in a state where we believe we can talk each other up. We put things down on a level with man and say that a preacher is a salesman; he is out selling the gospel. I have even heard people talk about gossiping the gospel. Gossip the gospel. I think that is hideous. I would not use it in a graveyard for a stray dog. I do not like that at all and do not tell me that the methods of God and winning man are the same method that a Fuller Brush salesman uses in selling a back scratcher.

The Holy Spirit operates on another realm altogether, and the method of winning a man to God is a divine method and not a human one. But we can make proselytes and church members, and get people over on our side, join in our class and go to our summer camp and have done nothing to him but make a proselyte out of him. But when the Holy Spirit works in a man, God does the work, and what God does the scripture says is forever. But we imagine we can handle it by the flesh and so we do handle it by the flesh, and the Lord lets us do it.

We can hold the Christian Creed, not know God, know the doctrine of the Church and not know spiritual things at all.

Another fearful consequence is that many people know about God but do not know God. There is a difference between knowing about God and knowing God.

I can know about your relative in Saskatchewan, but not know him, never have met him, never know the touch of his hand or the look of his eyes, the smile of his face or the sound of his voice, only know about him. You can even show me his picture and describe the man to me and still I do not know the man, I just know about the man.

A scientist, for instance, knows bugs. He writes books on bees, on worms, other bugs and various kinds of creatures.

Faber never knew a bug. He never could get through to them. You can know all about your dog and never know your dog. He will smile at you, stick his red tongue out and pant. He seems intelligent, but he is a dog and you have no organ, no technique for getting into his world. Externally you can comb him, wash him and feed him, clean his ears; you can know him externally, but you never can know your dog and your dog can never know you. He can know about you. He can know when you are glad and when you are angry with him and know when he has done the right thing and the wrong thing. Sometimes I think a dog has a conscious almost as good as people, but still the dog dies and never knows the man.

You can know about God, you can know about Christ dying for you, and you can even write songs and sell them. Anybody can write them. I could write a yard of hymns between now and midnight, after church service and sell them. However, I would not do it. I would not be caught dead doing it, too many people are doing it now. But you can write hymns, you can write books, you can head this and be the President of that and found this religious thing and still never know God at all, because only by the Holy Ghost can we know God.

Another consequence with this error is that we have two Christs. The Christ of history and of creed and of story and song. The Christ we sing about, the man upstairs or the Baby Jesus. Then there is the Christ, which the Spirit reveals. You never can piece Jesus together out of historic knowledge. You can read your New Testament and still never find Christ in it. You can be convinced that He is the Son of God and still never find Christ. The Holy Ghost reveals Christ.

A revelation of the Holy Spirit in one glorious flash of inward illumination will teach you more of Jesus than five years in a theological seminary. However, I believe in the seminaries. We ought to read everything we can read about Him, for reading about Him is legitimate and good and a part of Christianity. But the Holy Spirit must do the final flash that introduces your heart to Jesus, or it is not done at all.

Remember this; you only know Jesus as well as the Holy Spirit is pleased to reveal Him to you, for He cannot be revealed any other way. Even Paul said, "Now know we Christ, no longer after the flesh." The church cannot know Christ except as the Spirit reveals Him.

One more consequence is the blunder that modern Orthodoxy, modern fundamentalism, can know God with our minds. The Christian life is conceived to be much like the natural life, only jollier and cleaner and more fun. So the faith of our fathers has been identified with a number of questionable things.

A further one is philosophy. The modern neo-intellectual movement that is trying to resurrect the church by means of learning is about as far off the track as it is possible to be. Because you do not go to philosophy to find out about the Lord Jesus.

The Apostle Paul happened to be one of the most intellectual men that ever lived. A consensus among a great many learned scholars was that St. Paul was one of the sixth greatest intellects that ever lived. I personally think maybe he was the wisest and greatest intellect that ever lived, barring of course our Savior whom we never classify with other men. Even Paul said, "When I came to you I came not with wise words of men's wisdom but in demonstration of the Spirit and the power."

If you are reasoned into Christianity, some wise fellow can reason you out of it. But if you come to Christ by a flash of the Holy Ghost so that by intuit, know that you are God's child. You will know it by the text, but you will know it also by the inner illumination of the Spirit. Nobody can ever reason you out of it again.

Up until I was maybe thirty-three or thirty-four years old, I read more books on atheism than I did on Christianity. I had my Schofield Bible, my hymnbook and a few other books, Andrew Murray, Thomas Merton, and a few others, but I educated myself as well as I could by reading books. I read the philosophy of all the great minds of great men; all those fellows that, many of them did not believe in God, and did not believe in Christ certainly. I read White's *Warfare of Science with Christianity* or *Christianity with Science*. If a man can read that and still say he is saved, his reasoning does not save him; the Holy Ghost in him that's telling him he's saved saves him. I used to read those books and I was a young fellow and did not know much and I do not yet, but they would take away all my reasons and reduce me to palpitating ignorance.

And any other way a man would just get down, walk out, close his Bible, toss it on the shelf and say now there goes another one that goes along with Santa Claus and Jack Frost and a few other things he used to believe in. But you know what I used to do after reading a chapter or two that I could not answer and have arguments that I possibly could not defeat? I would get down on my knees and with tears; I would thank God with joy that no matter what they say, "Lord, I know Thee my Savior and my Lord." I did not have it in my head, I had it in my heart, and there is a difference there you see. If we have it in our head then of course philosophy will help us; if we have it in our heart there is not much philosophy can do except stand reverently, hat in hand, and say, "Holy, Holy, Holy is the Lord God Almighty."

Next, there is science. Science is called upon to prove Christianity. We just came through one of those long tunnels, when the evangelical church was running to science to get some sort of help, not knowing that everything that is divine in Christianity is exactly what science has no technique for investigating. The thing science can investigate is not divine, and the thing that is divine science cannot investigate. Science can make sputniks and science can make tape recorders. Science can do those things, but all that is nothing. Christianity is a miracle, a wondrous thing out of heaven, something let down like Peter's sheet, not depending upon the world or being a part of the world. It is something from the throne of God, like the waters of Ezekiel's vision. And science knows nothing about that. Science stands back, looks it over and does not know what to say. If we do not have this inner intuition, if we do not have this miraculous thing, then we run to science.

And the poor preachers, God help them; have tried over the last few years to prove miracles. They want to believe the miracles. I believe them all, but I do not believe them because science permits me; I believe them because God wrote them in the Bible and they are there. But some fellow finds a fish washed up on the shore and he measures its gullet. Gets himself a tape measure and craws inside the bony skeleton and measures its gullet and finds out it is as broad as the shoulders of a man and he goes out and says see, a great fish could swallow Jonah. See, the unbeliever is wrong; God did make a fish big enough to swallow Jonah.

Why go to tape measures and fish to find out whether what God says is true or not? If God did the thing, I could believe that.

Two scientists were walking down the street and one of them said, "You know that we have investigated, we have searched into and we weighed and measured, and we have found that the story of the donkey speaking is all false. The larynx of a donkey could not possibly articulate human speech."

Finally, a Scotsman had all he could take; so he went up and he said, "Mon, you make a donkey and I'll make him talk."

There you have it brother, if God can make a donkey He can make him talk. Christianity stands or falls on Jesus Christ. Stands or falls on the illumination of the Holy Ghost. Peter could have reasoned until the cows came home and not known anything. Immediately when the Holy Ghost came on him, he jumped up and said, "God has made this man Jesus be crucified, Lord and Christ." He knew by the Spirit that it was God.

Whole literature has grown up around the notion that Christianity may be proved by the fact that great men believe in Christ. If we can get a hold of a politician that believes in Christ, why we get him all over the front of our magazines and say, "Senator so and so believes in Christ;" and the implication is that if he believes in Christ, then Christ must be all right. When did Jesus Christ have to ride in on the coattail of a Senator?

You find some half-converted cowboy from that Sodom and Gomorrah called Hollywood, California; get him to say a nice thing about Jesus, go to the microphone and say everybody ought to go to Sunday school. Immediately it breaks into print and all poor dumb fundamentalists print his testimony. When did Jesus Christ have to come in on the testimony of a half-converted actor? No, no, my brother; Jesus stands alone. Let all the Senators and all the Presidents and all the Kings and Queens and Lords and Ladies of the world, along with all the great athletes and great actors, let them kneel at his feet and cry, "Holy, Holy, Holy, is the Lord God Almighty." Only the Holy Ghost can do this my brethren. For that reason, I do not bow down to great men. I bow down to the great Man. And if you have learned to worship one Man, you will not worship other men.

So, it is either the Holy Spirit or darkness. The Holy Spirit is God's imperative of life. And if our faith is to be a New Testament faith, if Christ is to be the Christ of God rather than the Christ of history, then the illumination of the Spirit

THE REALM OF THE SPIRIT

will tell our hearts and we are learning at the feet of Jesus, not at the feet of men.

Your knowledge of God is not taught to you from without; it is received by an inner anointing. You do not get your witness from a man; you get your witness from an inner anointing.

We have the mind of Christ. That is simple. Ah, what are we going to do now? Are we going to go home and argue about this and talk it over, say it was good or say it wasn't good or say it was too long or too short or whatever? Or are we going to do something about it? That is what bothers me. Are we going to do something about this? Are you going to open the door of your personality? Are you going to swing it wide? And you do not have to be afraid, as I have said before, for the Holy Spirit is an illuminator. He is light to the inner heart. And He will show you more of God in a moment than you can ever learn in a lifetime without Him. Then, when He does come, all that you have learned and all that you do learn will have its proper place in your total personality and total creed and total thinking, so you will not loose anything that you have learned. And He will not throw out what you have learned if it is truth, but He will set it on fire. He will add fire to the altar.

How He waits to be honored, the blessed Holy Spirit. He waits to be honored and He will honor Christ as we honor Christ. He waits. And if you will throw open your heart to Him, a new sun will rise on you. I know that by personal experience. Some time maybe I will tell you. It is a sacred thing and I do not often tell it. Moreover, if there is anything God has done through me, it dates back to that solemn, wondrous hour; when the light that was never on land or sea, the light that lighteth every man that cometh into the world, slashed in on my darkness. There was not conversion; I had been converted, soundly converted. It was subsequent to conversion. How about you?

CHAPTER 9

# The Gifts of the Spirit

THE APOSTLE PAUL WAS COMPELLED to write a letter, which he did what he said with boasting, he talked like a fool. But he did it in order that the people at Corinth would believe in him and would not think that he was a fanatic or false teacher. He said he was nobody but he did have to talk.

I am to talk about the gifts of the Spirit. If you were scared, you would not do that. Because there are two sides. You would be afraid if you got out of one side, you would get the others against you; and if you got out of the other, you would get the first ones against you. I guess it is the Irish in me, but I do not mind that at all. I do not care who is against me as long as God is on my side.

1 Corinthians 12: "Now concerning spiritual gifts brethren, I would not have you ignorant. Ye know that ye were Gentiles carried away with these dumb idols even as ye were led. Wherefore I give you to understand that no man speaking by the Spirit of God calleth Jesus accursed and that no man can say that Jesus is Lord but by the Holy Ghost. Now there are diversities of gifts but the same Spirit. And there are differences of administrations, but the same Lord. And there are diversities of operations, but it is the same God which worketh all in all. But the manifestation of the Spirit is given to every man to profit withal. For to one is given by the Spirit the word of

137

wisdom; to another the word of knowledge, to another faith by the same Spirit, to another the gifts of healing by the same Spirit, to another the working of miracles; to another prophecy; to another the discerning of spirits; to another divers kinds of tongues; to another the interpretation of tongues: But all these worketh that one and the selfsame Spirit dividing to every man severally as He will. For as the body is one and hath many members, and all the members of that one body, being many, are one body: so also is Christ. For by one Spirit are we all baptized into one body, whether we be Jews or Gentiles, whether we be bond or free; and have all been made to drink into one Spirit."

Then follows an explaining of the body of Christ and making it parallel between the members of our bodies; hands, and feet, and eyes, and so on.

And on over in 1 Corinthians 12: "Now ye are the body of Christ, and members in particular. And God hath set some in the church, in the body, first apostles, secondarily prophets, thirdly teachers, after that miracles, then gifts of healings, helps, governments, diversities of tongues. Are all apostles? are all prophets? are all teachers? are all workers of miracles? Have all the gifts of healing? do all speak with tongues? do all interpret?"

The answer of course is no. It is a rhetorical question.

Then in the book of Ephesians, the 4th chapte: "But unto every one of us is given grace according to the measure of the gift of Christ. Wherefore he saith, When he ascended up on high, he lead captivity captive and gave gifts unto men. He that descended is the same also that ascended up far above all heavens, that he might fill all things. And he gave some apostles, and some prophets, and some evangelists and some pastors and teachers. For the perfecting of the saints, for the work of the ministry, for the edifying of the body of Christ. Till all come in the unity of faith, and of the knowledge of the Son of God."

Twelth of Romans: "For I say through the grace given unto me to every man that is among you not to think of himself more highly than he ought to think; but to think soberly, according as God hath dealt to every man the measure of faith. For as we have many members in one body, and all members have not the same office, so we being many are one body in Christ and every one members one of another. Having then gifts differing according to the grace that is given to us, whether prophecy, let us prophesy, or ministry let us wait on our ministering or he that teacheth, on teaching. Or he that exhorteth, on exhortation, he that giveth, let him do it with simplicity, he that ruleth, with diligence he that sheweth mercy, with cheerfulness."

Here is the body of Christ and Paul draws a parallel. Paul was a great illustrator; he broke things down for us so we could get them. He said that the church was a body, that Christ was the head and that the true Christian is a member of that body; and all true Christians are part of the body, are members, are organs of that body. You will have a body beautifully equipped; nothing perhaps in the whole wide world is as beautifully made as the human body. The Holy Spirit said to David, "we are fearfully and wonderfully made." The hands, the eyes, the ears, the sense of smell, the sense of taste, the sense of touch and all feet and hands all working together.

The Holy Spirit is to the church what your spirit is to that body which God has given you. Each member recapitulates the local church. Paul in three epistles researched this. He uses the body-member relationship three times in Romans, First Corinthians and Ephesians. And he says that each local church recapitulates the entire church.

When the day of Pentecost was fully come they were all in one place. But that was the last time the whole church could all get in one place. Never been possible since. And the whole church cannot get in one place now for the reason that we are scattered all over the whole world; and I suppose that about 75 percent of the church or 85 percent of the church is already dead and in heaven. Therefore, it is impossible for them all to get together. So that if we had to have the whole church, from Paul and the apostles down to the newest convert saved tonight in a Rescue Mission; if we had to have them all together and in one place, you could not have a church at all. So that each local church recapitulates the entire church so that the church is not torn or divided; each local church group has all the functions of the whole group.

Just as the Province of Ontario is a living organic part of the whole federal government of Canada and just as my state of Pennsylvania is a living throbbing part of whole union of states, so each local church is not a political part, as the illustration would indicate but a living organic part of the whole Church of Christ. You see, I am a little bit Anglican; they go in a big way for the communion of saints. Well, brethren, so do I. I do not believe in communicating with the saints above but I believe in the communion with the saints. I believe that we are members of the whole body of Christ in heaven and in earth and just as a family.

Take our own family, my wife's family and mine. Seven of them, now multiplied sixteen more. Well they are all over the United States and California, to Maine and from Florida to Illinois, and yet they are all members of that same family. And we are the ancestors, and they have our name and appearance and look, and they all act the same and rest. Now the dear church of God is scattered all over the world and in heaven, but they are all descendants of the great God who, by the Holy Ghost and the word, caused them to be born into this family.

Therefore, the church is not divided. When we sing that old song, "We are not divided all one body we," people smile and say how about your 600 denominations. You cannot scare me, brother, so do not try it. We are not divided, "all one body we." That is just as true as I am not divided.

I have never had anything cut out yet. I am just keeping my fingers crossed and looking to God that nobody will ever get at me with a butcher knife. But up to now, I am all in one piece. I have not been taken apart. Nothing has been cut off and thrown out for the cats; I am all here. Consequently, the body of Christ is all one body, all one body we. We can sing it and let the people make fun of us if they will; keep on singing it for it's true. You are not divided. The whole church, everybody that is born into the family of God, is born into a living organic union, and there we are and there is nothing the devil can do about it.

Now, each local group I say has all the functions of the whole group; just as each man has all of his faculties and organs, members, and the members are designed, each for a function. As the eye is designed to see, the ear to hear, the hand to do work, the foot carry around, the stomach to digest your food and so on. So we are designed to cooperate and act in concert.

I remember once reading a great article in Harper's Magazine. I let it get away from me, and I cannot be sorrier about anything of that sort as I am about this. It explained what brought on old age. It was not the lose of strength in any organ of the body, but that the organs of the body cease to cooperate and went off on their own. That is what brought on old age and what made people die of old age; it was the failure of the organs of the body to cooperate. They got independent, went off and started their own tabernacle. When a fellow gets about sixty-five you know, his stomach says: I do not believe in pastors and official boards local churches, and I am going to go off on my own. So he goes off on his own and next thing you know, he has cancer of the stomach; and so it is with other members of the body. If they would all function together, you would stay young forever. But after a while, they break off and start out on their own and then you have trouble.

So it is with the church. When we are together and have a sense of unity and fellowship; and all work together, cooperate with each other, and act in concert, all for each and each for all; and all take direction from the head, and then you will have the perfect church. We have never had that on earth yet after the very early times; probably will not have it again, but each local church can sum it up. I use the word recapitulate. I thought some young fellow would not know what I meant; and I will say, we can all sum it up in ourselves so that anything that God can do through all of His church, He can do through the local crowd, local group, local church.

Now what these various functions are, are these: They are the abilities to work and are called gifts. And He said having these gifts differ for you according to grace. "Now concerning spiritual gifts brethren, covet earnestly the best gift. When He ascended up on high, He gave gifts." So the gifts when lodged in the body of Christ in the local church are the ability to do. What is your stomach? Your stomach is a gift from God. What is the purpose of it? Not to hold your trousers up; it is not for that. You put a belt around. It is there for a purpose. It has a function there. What is your liver for? What is your eye for? They are all there for a purpose. They have a function, something to do; and if they do it right and all the others cooperate, you will be a healthy strong person.

So here, we have these gifts in the church. Paul, in his carefully thought out and carefully God inspired writings, explained these gifts were there to get things done. They are there for a purpose. Just as in baseball; now Paul used sports to illustrate, and I will use sports to illustrate, so do not say I am not spiritual. I have no ambition to be more spiritual that the Apostle Paul. I do not know anything about hockey so I will take baseball. You know that on a team of nine men, there is mostly more, but they are spares. Nine main men; there's the batter, the fellow to catch the ball, the fellow to pitch the ball, there's a fellow in the center field to catch it if the fellow who's batting hits it, and there's the fellow on first base, second base; they all have their function. Everybody knows what he is supposed to do. And as long as he does that and does it skillfully, it would be a hard team to beat.

Whenever they get a star who doesn't care whether the teams wins or not provided we can shine, then you don't have a good team.

Paul says that these gifts are in the body. Mostly we say that there are nine of them. That is because 1 Corinthians, in the opening verses, lists nine; but you know that I have counted at least eighteen. Maybe there could be some that overlap and that they use synonyms, in which case, maybe it could be reduced to fifteen. But let me follow in the scriptures closely now. I am not using my imagination, I am staying by the word of God. Let me name the organs of the divine body which are named by Paul in the passages which I read.

First there is the gift of the apostle or an ambassador or messenger; then there's a gift that makes a prophet, then there's the gift that makes a teacher, then there's the gift that makes an exhorter; then there is the gift that makes the ruler, that would be someone the old Presbyterian's call the ruling elder; then there's the gift of wisdom, gift of knowledge, gift of faith; gift of healing, gift of miracles; gift of tongues, gift of interpretations, gift of discernment; gift of helps, gift of mercy showing, the gift of government; the gift of giving, liberality, and the gift of the evangelist. Now there you have it. Those are the gifts, which are in the body. Now, if you cared to do it, and wanted to go into it, you could start and name the organs of the body, just as I have named eighteen organs of the body of Christ. Eighteen things, which enable the Holy Spirit to work. As long as you have the body members, the life within you can find its way out. If you are a musician, your hands are nothing. They don't know anything at all; there they are, cut them off and they're completely dead. But as long your hands are obedient to the head you might be able to play the piano, or something else if you like it. Just as long as your eye takes orders from the head, your eye will be all right. As long as your feet take orders from your head, you will not be hit when you cross the street. Just as long as the members of your body work and take orders from the head, you will be all right.

And just as long as the Church of Christ recognizes the Lord as being the head of the church, and the Christians and members in particular and these members are gifted with abilities to do, then we will have a revived and blessed church. But you see there are two mistakes that have been made, and I will talk about those two mistakes a little bit later, about these gifts of the Spirit.

Now the Spirit working through these gifts and through these gifted members does the work of the church. For if these gifts are not present, are not recognized or denied, the church is thrown back upon getting the work done. If you did not have any hands, then you would have to do the best you could without any hands. I have seen men afflicted without any hands. If you did not have any eyes, you would have to do the best you could without eyes. If you had no feet, you would have to crawl around as best you could with out feet. Therefore, if we deny or refuse to recognize that there are members and that there are gifts in those members, then we are thrown back upon humanism.

And here is what we have today, and we have an awful lot of it. We are thrown back upon talent, just talent; that is a good theatrical word but we are thrown back upon it. Let me solemnly tell you, ladies and gentlemen, the Holy Ghost never works with mere talent. Do not be mistaken by the parable of Jesus with the word talent; there it meant a sum of money. It had no reference of whether you could sing or imitate or whatever the theatrical people do.

Or we are thrown back on psychology. I am somewhat amused and downright disgusted with some of my ministerial brethren of the cloth, who are so busy studying psychology in order that they may know how to handle their congregations. How silly can you get? When you have a Bible and a mouth, and the Holy Ghost, why do you have to study psychology? It just so happens that when I was a young fellow in my twenties, I was a great student of psychology. I studied Watson, Jennings and particularly Freud, who was the pappy of psychiatry and psychoanalysis. I learned all the terms and all of that so I know about it. I am not dumb about psychology, but there is no use to bring psychology to the pulpit when you have the Holy Ghost. If you have the gift of the Spirit, you do not need to study Freud. You can study him all right; I do not say do not study him, but do not bring him into the pulpit with you. Just the same as you can have an automobile or a radio or a camera, but do not bring it into the pulpit. Get up and trust God.

Another technique is business methods. I get amused somewhat and hurt a little about the brethren and their business methods; trying to carry on the work of God after the fashion of the American business man. So we carry on as they do in Madison Avenue or Wall Street. It will not work brethren, just as sure as you let it, it will not work. It is all artificial limbs, it will not work.

Then political techniques and sales methods: That is what we are up against; we got that in church now. We are going to have to restudy this whole business in place of the Holy Spirit in the church, in order that the church can operate again.

If the life goes out of a man's body, he is said to be a corpse. He is what they call the remains. It is sad, but almost humorously sad, that a man can walk around strong, fine man with shining eyes and vibrant voice; a living man, and then he dies, and we say the remains can be seen at such and such funeral home. The remains, all that remains of the man, and the least part about him, is what you can see there in the funeral home. But the living man is gone. You have only the body left and the body is the remains.

So it is in the Church of Christ. It is literally true that some churches are dead; the Holy Ghost is gone out of them and all you have left is the remains. You have the potential there of the church, but you do not have the church. Because just as you have in a dead man, you have the potential of a living man, but you do not have the living man. He cannot talk, he cannot taste, he cannot touch, he can not feel, he cannot smell, he cannot hear, he cannot see because he is dead. The soul has gone out of the man, and when the Holy Spirit is not present in the church, you have to get along after the methods of business or politics or psychology or something else. Not too much can be said, my friend, about the necessity of the Holy Ghost in the church, not too much.

Now, we can get off down the back alley and be fanatical about it, but you cannot say too much about it if you say stay with the scripture. For without the Spirit there can be nothing done for eternity. Well, then somebody would say, "Mr. Tozer, then if that's true, then here is where you have to pray, because some of my dear friends would stomp out and prove how spiritual they are by never coming back."

Why is it that we do not cast our lot in with the tongues movement because they believe this? Well now, I have known and studied these dear brethren. I've preached to them for a long, long time and I've studied them; and I know them pretty well, and I'm very sympathetic with them; and I love them, and in all love and charity, I'd like to say they are some good sweet Christians among them. And I happen to know some dear, beloved, sweet Christians that are in this movement. Also, there are some churches that are very sane, beautiful, godly and good, but a number of things that I want to name have characterized the movement itself.

I do not want to hurt anybody's feelings; and if you think this is not true, then you can call me up, come to see me, bring your proof. If it's true, and as Christians and members of the body of Christ, we've all got to smile and say thank God for the truth no matter whether it hurts or not. The movement itself has done this. It has magnified one single gift above all others and that one gift, as Paul said, was the least. Now, that does not cause me to have great confidence in the movement that would do that. Then there is an unscriptural exhibition of that gift, which incidentally began in the United States about 1904.

## CHAPTER 10

# Don't Beg God for the Holy Spirit

CONTRARY TO WHAT MOST PEOPLE MIGHT ASSUME, the important thing about the day of Pentecost was not that the Spirit had come. The important thing was that Jesus had been exalted. He said Himself, in that last great day of the feast in Jerusalem some time before, that whoever believed in Him out of his inmost being there shall flow rivers of living water, but this spake ye of the Spirit, which they that believed in Him ought to receive. The Spirit had not been given because Jesus had not yet been glorified. The glorification of Jesus brought the Holy Ghost.

Now we ought to be able to get a hold of that instantly, that wherever Jesus is glorified, the Holy Spirit comes. He need not be begged; He comes when the Savior is glorified, when Christ is honored.

The verse I want to get particularly to is this one: But Peter stood up and lifted up his voice. He stood up and lifted up his voice. Peter here stands for the whole church of God. Peter was the first man to get on his feet after the Holy Spirit had come to his church. And as far and as long as the church has been the true church, and wherever it is the true church, the individual believes the Lord's Word. Peter had believed the Lord's Word and he received confirmation in his own breast.

I wrote a series of articles that became a little booklet. In it, I had one chapter in which I said: the difference between faith as it was found in the New Testament and faith as it is found now is that, faith in the New Testament produced something and there was a confirmation of it. Faith now is a beginning and an end. We have faith in faith but nothing happens. They had faith in a risen Christ; something happened, and that is the difference.

Here was Peter standing up and he lifted up, and that was the business of the church. Peter became a witness as the church is a witness on earth as things in heaven. The church is a witness of powers beyond the earthly and the human. It is a source of great grief to me that the church is trying to run on its human powers. Peter testified that something beyond the human and beyond the earthly; some power that lay beyond the earthly scene, that was interested in us men and women; and not only that, but was working in men and women and willing to enter us and make itself known to us.

The kind of Christianity prominent today does not know where it is and is trying to run a heavenly institution after an earthly manner. Now if this church is to be a church of Christ, a living organic member of that redeemed body of which Christ is the Head, then it's teachers and it's members must strive earnestly and sacrificially and with constant prayer do a number of things. Let me name them for you; the church and all the churches of all the denominations that are gospel churches, whether we are all a part of the same body.

If we are to be that kind of church, then there are certain things that we must do. Not nibble at, but earnestly strive to do, sacrificially and with constant earnest prayer. We must strive to make our practices New Testament in their content. Nothing dragged in from the outside, but we must teach and do New Testament truths, and we must constantly go to the grassroots.

The founders of this great North American continent took over a wilderness and made it into a civilized continent. How did they do it? They did it by going out with their axes, cutting down the trees first and making houses, and then planting corn and potatoes and other vegetables and grains; and when they planted, they didn't go back home to bed and sleep until time to harvest it. They fought the intrusion from the wilderness from the day they planted their corn and the rest of their crops, until they harvested them and had them safely in their log barns. The wilderness encroaches on the fruitful fields requiring constant fighting.

As a farm boy from the state of Pennsylvania, I know how we used to have to do; plant your corn, then cross your fingers, pray and then get your shotgun out; because the crows would have your corn if you did not do everything that was possible to do. Now it is the same with the church.

One of the old saints said, "Never think for a minute that there is a time when you won't be tempted, and he is tempted the most effectively who thinks he is not being tempted at all." Just when you think you are not being tempted, that is the time when you are being tempted the most effectively. Therefore, it is with the church. We lean back on our own laurels and say that may be true of some churches, but it is not true of us. We are increased with goods and have need of nothing. However, I want to remind you that you have to fight for what you have. This little field of God's planting has to have plenty of shotguns and plenty of watchmen driving off crows. Not only crows, but also bears and foxes and groundhogs and all sorts of other creatures, to say nothing of the little insects that destroy crops. You have to keep after them. You have to keep your field healthy. There is only one way to do it and that is to keep it true to the Word. Keep the Word in it, constantly going back to the grassroots and getting the Word into the church.

And we must not only do this, but we must also earnestly, sacrificially and prayerfully strive to be empowered with that same power that came upon them; Whom Peter said God has shed forth this, which ye now see and hear. And to live the life of heaven here upon the earth. And to put loyalty to Christ first at any cost. Now that is a church and nothing else is a church. I personally want to be a member of that church. I'd rather be in a little room over a barbershop on a side street somewhere with twenty people meeting and singing off key some old hymn of Zion than to be a part of a great going concern that is not New Testament in its doctrine, in its Spirit, in its living, in its holiness and all of its whole texture and tenor.

We must be New Testament, and of course such a church as that need not expect to be relatively popular. But certain truths will follow it if we make our church that kind of church. Certain people will follow it. Its people would be a joyful people. When the Holy Ghost came upon the Moravians in 1727, that October, that morning when they were having communion. They said when they went out of that place scarcely knowing whether they were on earth or had died already and gone to heaven. And that was the characteristic of the Moravians for a hundred years. The characteristic was joy, they were joyful people. They were not a happy people in the sense that they worked up their happiness, they were a joyful people. The joy came from within.

Well now, brethren, listen to me. I say when we give God His place in the church, when we recognize Christ as Lord, high and lifted up, when we give the Holy Spirit His place, there will be a joy that is not worked up. It will be a joy that springs like a fountain. The Lord said it should be a fountain, an artesian well that springs up from within. So that will be one characteristic of a Spirit-filled church. There will be a joyful people and it will be easy to distinguish them from the children of the world. I wonder what Paul would say if he came down and looked us over; up and down the aisles and looked us over. Then went down to a theater and looked them over. Then went to a hockey game and looked them over, then went down and looked at the people shopping, then went out on the street and wherever crowds were, and then came back and looked us over. I don't think he would see very much difference really.

A church that is Spirit-filled will be useful to the race of man. We ought to be useful to the race of men. Some claim preachers are parasites. The Communists say we are, and a lot of others. They say we are social parasites, that we do not turn a hand to earn anything; we just live like a parasite.

Back on the farm, our dog used to come in flapping his long ears and whining. My father would say he has a tick in his ear and they would hunt for it. A tick is a little flat insect that jumps on a dog's ear and drinks blood until he is a puffed up, full of dog blood. You have to pull that off and the head pops off and it gets sore. It is a mess.

Anyhow, they say we are parasites; we drink the blood of society and do not produce a thing. I have seven children and sixteen grandchildren. That is not so bad. The scripture says to me that the ox that works in the cornfield, you feed him, it says. That is my version. It says to feed the ox so; they do not get me down talking about like that. I know how God does things.

If I was driving a truck, for instance, how could I preach sermons on Sundays? So the Lord says, "I have a lot of truck drivers, you get me a room and get quiet there and read and sing and get up sermons and talk to the people and I'll talk to you." I am not worried about what they say about us being parasites.

I believe the church ought to be useful to the whole community. Because we are here, everybody ought to be better. You can help the neighborhood where you live; you can help this neighborhood, and the neighborhood should be better because we are here. And we do not need to apologize; they owe us money, they owe us a great debt. They can rob us but we keep the crime rate down, nevertheless.

If you have more God-filled, Spirit-filled churches you could have less cops on the street. Be sure of that; where there is Godliness there is less crime. A Spirit-filled church is useful to the neighborhood, useful to the sons of men, even the ones that are not converted; and it will be influential among the churches. I would like to see this church become so godly, so Spirit-filled, that it would have a spiritual influence on all the churches in the whole city. That everybody in this city, every church in this city, would have to take off its hat and stand at attention. I am not unspiritual in this because Paul told some of his people, "your Godliness and faith is talked about through all Asia Minor." It is entirely right that I could hope this in you, that I hope that we might become so Spirit-filled, walk with God, learn to worship and live so clean and so separated that everybody will know it and other churches in the city would be blessed because of it.

When Luther had his reformation, the Catholic Church was forced to clean up just because the moral pressure from Lutheranism forced the Roman church to clean up. And when Wesley came and preached, the Anglican Church was forced to clean up some of the things that were wrong with them. That is not to speak unkindly of my Anglican friends because I have many of them. It has only to say that in those times they needed some help. Methodism was a spiritual force that compelled them to do something about their own condition.

There is no reason why we could not be a people here so filled with the Spirit, so joyfully, singing His praises and living so clean in our business and home and school that the people would know it; and other churches would be forced to straighten up and clean up and begin to pray for something too, because we'd set the standard for them. Whenever you have a Spirit-filled people, you have a people that can live well and die well. "Oh, these people die well," they said of the Methodist. "Behold how these people die," said a man as he looked at the martyrs in the old Roman days. If you live well you will die well.

Old Balaam wanted to die the death of the righteous, but he would not live the life of the righteous. If you are going to die the death of the righteous, you must live the life of the righteous. And a Christian ought to be able to die well; they should be able to do that if nothing else.

There are some who won't feel at home in a church like that; and if you're hope is to have everybody and his brother on his mother's side to just come sit around and glow, just put that out of your head, brother. It just will not happen that way. Not all men have faith. There are just some people that do not want that kind of church, and I will name them now.

The people who put on religion as a Sunday garment, their well-pressed Sunday garment. So if this comes and we do get the help we need from God why those who merely make religion a Sunday garment, they will not like it very well. Because we will insist they live right on Monday morning and they do not want to do that. And they that keep their religion disengaged from practical living, they will not like it either You know, they will disengage their religion. Some people have a wonderful way of disengaging. Their religion is here, they are living here, and on Sundays, they go and polish off their religion. Then evening about eleven o'clock they put it on the shelf, and then Monday they go out and live like they want to live. Now nobody like that likes to hear me preach. Nobody. If you like that, you will not want to hear me preach. I won't surrender to that kind of thing, and I won't surrender to that kind of people; and I wouldn't care if it was the whole Senate of the United States and the Parliament of Canada, and all the big doctors and scientists, and all the great nabobs in the whole continent said they'd come and join my church. I'd still preach the same thing because we ought to be a church of the living God and not a gathering of big shots necessarily; though the big shots can come, if they will get on their knees; and if a big shot is on their knees, they are not taller than anyone else you know. Did you ever think of that?

Furthermore, there are those who refuse to let religion endanger them in any way. They refuse to let it interfere with their pleasure or their plans. They will serve Jesus and go to heaven, are saved and cannot loose their light; so they will make it through, you know; but they are going to have fun on the way there. They lay their lives out just as a gardener lays out the garden or a woman, sometimes my wife cuts out a pattern; lays out a pattern on the table and it looks like a mess to me, but it turns out to be a dress for the granddaughter. And we lay out our lives, you know; and we say now, "it's nice to serve thee and we love thee Lord and let's sing a chorus;" but we won't change that pattern any, we're going to keep that pattern. But the cross of Jesus Christ always changes that path, always gets in there and makes a man change his life.

The Cross of Christ is revolutionary. And if we are not ready to let it be revolutionary in us, we are not going to like a church that takes the things of God seriously and let it cost us anything, control us in any way. People want the benefit of the Cross but they do not want the control of the Cross. They want all that the Cross can offer but they do not want to be under the Lordship of Jesus.

Of course, there are those who expect religion to be fun. We have just gone through a long period when Christianity was the funniest thing on the continent. You could have more fun serving Jesus than doing anything else in the whole world. It was clean too; you did not have a hangover. You go down to a corner pub, and have a good time but you will have a hangover. They say, "Do you serve Jesus, you can have all the fun you want to and you will not have a hangover."

That kind of Christianity for the sake of fun, Christianity as an entertaining medium. The whole thing is offensive and foul before God Almighty. My brother, the cross of Christ is not fun and it never was fun. There is such a thing as the joy of the Lord, which is strength to the people. There is such a thing as having joy unspeakable and full of glory, but there is also such a thing as dying while we grieve. The idea that Christianity is another form of entertainment is perfectly ridiculous.

I wrote one time something and said Christianity would not make a form of entertainment. A fellow felt called to write and answer me. He was editor of a magazine, and wrote me up in his magazine. I said something to the effect that we ought not to see things, but that we ought to see the things that were invisible. He noticed it and wrote, "Tozer believes in going to church and keeping your eyes shut." Well of course, he did not understand what I was talking about. Or perhaps he did understand but was lying about it. Then he said, "Tozer was all wet and ought to know better," he said, "every time you sing a hymn you're being entertained."

Maybe he was, but brother, I am not. When I sing, "Amazing Grace how sweet the sound," I am worshipping God Almighty. If you want to call that which they do before the throne when they cry day and night without ceasing "holy, holy, holy, Lord God Almighty" and hide their face behind their wings, if that is entertaining, then I am an entertainer.

But if it is not, and it is not, then I am a worshipper. Nobody ever worshipped God then went out and committed suicide as a hangover. Many a man has killed himself because he had just burnt himself out trying to have fun. Then a pretty young lady goes out, throws herself into having fun and before she's twenty-five years old, she's an old hag and has to have a retread job done on her countenance before anybody can look at her without gagging. She has simply burnt herself out. She has defeated and burnt herself out. Everywhere you go you find it.

All these pretty actresses you see and see their pictures, some of you have gone to see them, well you ought to see them when they get up in the morning. Brother they have to have a patch job done on their face before they dare even come down to breakfast. All burnt out. I love to see the grace of God in a face, don't you?

I was among the Brethren in Christ; those clean people who have all these things and all and women have little black hats sitting up on top of their head, and their hair is done up in a bun here, and their ears stick out, and I preached for them. I was blessed, just wonderfully and absolutely blessed. They did not have a thing on but faith; not a thing on their head but hair, and a little black thing for the angels, according to 1 Corinthians. They covered their head for the sake of the angels and they were just sweet, you know. Look at them and they remind you of your dead old aunt back in Pennsylvania, or your grandmother out in New Brunswick; and you think of all the nice people you ever knew; the sweet good people you ever knew, when you look at them. You do not have to apologize for them; just nice people, the Brethren in Christ.

I could not join them but I do admire them tremendously. I had a tie on and I told the President of the college where I was, "I'm a Gentile and I don't know whether they'll take me in or not."

He said, "Preach to their hearts and they'll forget that you don't belong to them."

I did just that and they did just that.

Of course, there are those who embrace religion for its cultural values. Did you ever meet those people? They do not know anything about a Spirit-filled life or the Spirit-filled church, but the cultural value of the church is good for them. They want their children brought up in the culture of the church. Anybody that does that, of course they are not going to be at home among God's dear people. They want book reviews and all that sort of thing. They will not be at home, but they will be some that will be at home, and I am going to name them and then quit for tonight. I know we want to sing and I am not going to press the length of my sermon unduly. But there will be some people if we have a Spirit-filled church that practices the belief of the New Testament: and goes constantly to the grassroots and roots out everything that isn't of God, keeps the green growing lush and beautiful into things heavenly and walks with God and obeys the truth and loves each other; we'll rule out a few but these will be in their glory.

Now who are they?

Those who have a leading ambition to get rid of their sins. If you have not gotten over a burdening ambition to get rid of your sins, you will not like to hear me preach very often or long. You will not do it because I believe we ought to want to be rid of our sins. If I had a cancer growing on my neck I would want to be rid of that thing, and no body could come to me and say, "Now here, I've got cow bell here, let me shake it. Don't you like it?" I would say, "No I do not like it, I'm interested in this cancer on my neck, have you got a cure for it?" He would say, "Let's forget the cancer, let me give you the bell, you can jingle the bell."

I would say, "I've heard real cowbells on real cows when I was on the farm and I don't want to hear them in the church. So get them out of here and let's talk about getting rid of your sins."

My brother, there are some people that are overwhelmed with the desire to get rid of their sins. Those people would be happy among us. To know and walk with God. Their only ambition is to walk with God and to follow the Lamb, wheresoever He goest. You know the Lord's people kind of know each other; they do, they know each other. You know, you may occasionally get a bad apple. Jesus had Judas Iscariot in His little flock. Mostly we know each other. When we shake hands and someone says something to you about God, you know you are talking to a brother in Christ, regardless of whether he is an Irishman or Scottish, or Englishman or American or what he may be; we all talk the same language and we are all brothers and sisters in Jesus Christ our Lord.

Those who have learned to recognize the voice of the Shepherd; they will be at home in the Spirit-filled church. Some people have never heard the voice of the Shepherd. Oh, that voice of the Shepherd, tender as a lullaby, strong as a wind and as mighty as the sound of many waters. The voice of Jesus, that healing, musical, solemn, beautiful voice of Jesus in His church. And the people who have learned to hear that voice can recognize it are always at home, where everything centers on Him. Jesus is all in all.

In the early days of the Christian and Missionary Alliance, we were a conglomeration of everything under the sun, and we still are; we really still are. That is we have Calvinists, Armenians, Methodists, Baptists, and all sorts of people and we're all together on one thing; Jesus Christ is wisdom, righteousness, sanctification, redemption; He's all in all. You know the people of the Lord who have learned to hear the voice of the Shepherd; they gravitated toward that sort of place.

Then there are those who are sensitive to the invisible presence. They are not so sure who else is present, but they know the Lord is present. They are sensitive to that. You're heart is sensitive to that, the Lord's presence. Or are you a sampler and a nibbler. Well God help you and bless you if you are, but a child of the King isn't a sampler and nibbler; he's a sheep who loves his Shepherd. He stays awfully close to the Shepherd.

The only safe place for a sheep is by the side of his shepherd, because the devil does not fear sheep; he just fears the Shepherd, that is all. Now not all the sheep in Ontario would be a match for one wolf. If you give a wolf time, he could eat all the sheep in Canada. Give him time and grant he would live long enough, he could do it, because they can't fight back you see. They just run and put their heads together and make funny pleading, beeping sounds. A wolf does not mind that and that is all God's people can do. So our safety lies in being near the Shepherd; stay close to Jesus and all the wolves in the world cannot get a tooth in you, thank God.

Well there are some who've tasted of the good Word of God and felt the mysterious power of the world to come. Have you, have you? If you have not, maybe it is because you are not doing anything about it. Maybe it is because you do not want this or do not want it enough.

But if there are those in church, are you present here tonight, would rather hear the voice of Jesus than to hear the voice of the greatest speaker or the best singer in the world; would rather be conscious of the divine, than to be conscious of the greatest man in the world; is sick of his sins and longs to be holy; then I'm preaching to you, and I pray that your numbers may increase, and I pray that you'll tell others this is what we stand for down the road. This is what I believe in: Jesus Christ, clean living; joyful, radiant, happy worship; good, sweet fellowship and kindliness; and patience and endurance and honesty; the missionary outlook and good decency and separation from all things that are wrong. Above all things, worship the Lord in the beauty of holiness, and learn to know the wondrous sound of the Shepherd's voice.

That is what we stand for, that is what we believe in. That is what we are preaching.

# Closing

THIS BOOK IS NOT TO BE READ as you would a novel. Moreover, Dr. Tozer would not want you to read this book and accept everything he says at face value. It would greatly disturb him to think you did that. He cast a jaundiced eye towards the comment, "the book was so interesting, I couldn't put it down until I read it all the way through." Such shallow reading was far from his ideal.

Tozer belonged to the school of thought that insisted that some books need to be slowly chewed and meditated on. Perhaps a paragraph, or even a word, would cause a person to stop reading and to spend time meditating and praying. Some books are supposed to be read on your knees, asking God to minister to your heart through the written word. I think this is one of them.

If you have read this book and closed it with the satisfaction of knowing that you have read another "Tozer book," you have missed the real significance of the ministry of this book. You should not agree with everything in this book. You should not assume that Dr. Tozer is right in his conclusions. He may very well be, but never assume he is correct. What he says in this book should do two things for us.

Number one, it should send us to our knees to examine our own heart.

Number two, it should send us to our Bible to make sure that what he is saying is absolutely what the Word of God teaches.

To come away from a book like this with a greater understanding of the topic is wonderful. However, to come away with a deeper surrender to the Holy Spirit is the whole purpose of this book.

In one of his books, Dr. Tozer makes this observation:

"It is important that we get still to wait on God. And it is best that we get alone, preferably with our Bible outspread before us. Then, if we will, we may draw near to God and began to hear Him speak to us in our hearts. I think for the average person the progression will be something like this: First a sound as of a Presence walking in the garden. Then a Voice, more intelligible, but still far from clear. Then the happy moment when the Spirit begins to illuminate the Scriptures; and that which had been only a sound, or at best a voice, now becomes an intelligible word; warm and intimate and clear as the word of a dear friend. Then will come life and light, and best of all, ability to see and rest in and brace Jesus Christ as Savior and Lord of all." (*The Pursuit of God*)

May God honor you by showing you the Mystery and Majesty of the Holy Spirit in your life and ministry.

# Study Guide

**CHAPTER 1:**

1. What was the blunder theological liberals in America made about a hundred years ago?

2. What is the Athanasian Creed about?

3. What is the relationship of the Holy Spirit to the Father and the Son?

4. What does the Holy Spirit think of sinful people?

**CHAPTER 2:**

1. What is the promise of the Father?

2. Name the three periods that are discernible with respect to the Holy Spirit in His work in the Church.

3. Was the Father's promise for the first century Christians only?

**CHAPTER 3:**

1. Is the power of the Holy Spirit necessary to make miracle workers?

2. What are some of the differences the Holy Spirit made to the disciples after Pentecost?

3. What happened to John Wesley at Aldersgate Street?

**CHAPTER 4:**

1. What can never be repeated again in Christianity?

2. What is the eternal meaning of Acts 2?

3. What is one of the major things wrong with our Christian services?

**CHAPTER 5:**

1. What do you think the Raven of Noah's Ark represented?

2. What is the dove of Noah's Ark a type and picture of?

3. What are some of the marks of God's displeasure upon His people?

**CHAPTER 6:**

1. Do you think every Christian wants to be filled with the Holy Spirit?

2. What are some of the reasons a Christian would *not* want to be filled?

3. What was King Agag a type of?

4. What are the four Scripture texts concerning being filled with the Holy Spirit?

**CHAPTER 7:**

1. For two to walk together voluntarily, what must they be?

2. What is the wrong reason why some people would like to be filled with the Holy Spirit?

3. Is the Holy Spirit a person or an influence? Explain your answer.

4. Can you be a Christian without being a disciple?

**CHAPTER 8:**

1. The realm of the Spirit is closed to what? Explain why.

2. Who said, "I think, therefore I am"? What do you think of that statement?

3. Explain the difference between knowing about God and knowing God.

**CHAPTER 9:**

1.  As a Christian, why should it not matter to you if everyone is against you?

2.  Finish this sentence: The Holy Spirit is to the church what your spirit is to _____.

3.  How many actual gifts of the Holy Spirit are there?

4.  Why is it that some churches are dead?

## CHAPTER 10:

1.  The Holy Spirit will come whenever what happens?

2.  What is the difference between faith as it was found in the New Testament and faith as it is found now?

3.  If you want to die the death of the righteous, what must you do?

4.  Are those who embrace religion for cultural or political values true Christians?

5.  Where is the only safe place for a sheep?

6.  Have you tasted of the good Word of God and felt the mysterious power of the world to come?

# Index

Enjoy this excerpt from our other Pure Gold Classic
by A.W. Tozer

## FELLOWSHIP OF THE BURNING HEART

# *Believing Prayer:*
## *Faith as Confidence in God*

John 14:13-14 (KJV) "*And whatsoever ye shall ask in my name, that will I do, that the Father may be glorified in the Son. If ye shall ask any thing in my name, I will do it.*"

1 John 5:14-15 (KJV). "*And this is the confidence that we have in him, that, if we ask any thing according to his will, he heareth us: And if we know that he hear us, whatsoever we ask, we know that we have the petitions that we desired of him.*"

THE FOCUS OF MY SUBJECT IS FAITH as confidence in God. This may have a familiar ring inasmuch as it will constitute my philosophy of faith and it is, among evangelicals, a theme we like to dwell on.

Let me say to begin that there is a great deal of praying being done that doesn't amount to anything. It never brings back anything to us. No possible good can come in trying to cover this up or deny it. We will do a great lot better by admitting that there is enough prayer made any Sunday to save the whole world, even four or five suburbs of the world. But the world isn't saved and much of our praying is the echo of our own voices.

This has a very injurious effect upon the Church of Christ—not only injurious but sometimes disastrous. Unanswered prayer does five things in a congregation over an extended period:

(1) It tends to chill and discourage the praying people. If we continue to ask like a petulant child that doesn't expect to get what it asks for but continues to whine for it, if we continue to do that and never get an answer, the temptation is that we will get chilled and cold inside our hearts and become discouraged.

(2) Then it confirms the natural unbelief of the heart. For, remember this – the human heart by nature is filled with unbelief. It was unbelief that led to the first act of disobedience. Therefore, not disobedience, but unbelief, was the first sin. While disobedience is the first recorded sin, in back of the act of disobedience, there was the sin of unbelief, or the disobedience never would have taken place.

Here is the danger as I see it. To pray and not receive an answer and to have a church pray and never see the answer is detrimental to solid spiritual growth. When we pray for the sick and have them not recover or even die, when we pray for deliverance and never see it, when we pray for a thousand things and never see one of them brought to pass, I say the effect is to confirm the natural unbelief in the human breast.

(3) Then it encourages the idea that religion is unreal. A great many people have the idea that religion is unreal. They believe it is a subjective thing purely and there is nothing real about it and there is nothing to which it can be referred. I use the word, "horse." Everybody's mind jumps to a large animal with short hair and ears that stand up, an intelligent face, fast on its feet, and powerful. Everybody knows what the word "horse" means because our English word "horse" has a reference – something to which the word refers.

I use the word "lake" and everybody thinks of a large body of water. I use the word "star" and everybody thinks of the heavenly bodies. But we can use the words "faith" and "belief" and "God" and "Heaven," and there is nothing to which they refer. They are just words. Like pixies and fairies and such things that have no referance in the real world.

(4) Then it gives plenty of occasions to the enemy to blaspheme. The enemy loves to blaspheme. He is a dirty-mouthed, obscene blasphemer. I don't like to even abuse the devil, but I have a lot of secret sympathy, though I wouldn't myself use it, but I have a lot of secret sympathy for that rough old Irishman, William Nicholson, who calls the devil a "dirrrty ole pig." And he is just that. He is an obscene old pig and he loves to blaspheme. And if he can get a lot of Christians howling to high heaven for weeks on end and see to it that they never get an answer, I don't know what he says, but I know what he says has more obscenities in it and he blasphemes God.

(5) Worst of all, it lets the enemy take possession of the field. In the failure of a military drive, the worst part is not the men they lose. The worst part is not the face they lose. The worst part of the failure of a military drive is that it leaves the enemy in possession of the field. And when the people of God pray and pray and get nowhere, it leaves the enemy in possession of the field.

This, in itself, is a tragedy and a disaster. The devil should be on the run. We should never see anything but the back of his neck. He should always be retreating and retreating, and his worst fighting should be rear-guard action, scorched-earth policy, burning, and destroying as he goes, but he should always be on the run. Instead of that, the obscene and blasphemous enemy smugly and scornfully holds his position, and the people of God let him have it. This, of course, retards the work of the Lord greatly.

Having no prayers answered—having prayers sent up to Heaven that come back empty—is like sending an army out without weapons. It like setting a pianist without fingers down to a piano. It is like sending a woodsman without an axe into the woods. It is like sending a farmer without a plough into the field. And the work of God stands still.

Now, Jesus said that we could have anything we ask in His name. John said that this is the confidence, the boldness, and the assurance. Our English tongue is a highly versatile, almost volatile tongue, and we can say anything we want to say. It is the richest of all the languages, because it has received tributaries from everywhere. But, our difficulty is that we sometimes have to use a half dozen words to mean as much as one word in another language. So, when the Holy Ghost said, "This is the confidence we have in Him," that English word "confidence" is not enough. So, the translators call it: "This is the boldness we have in Him." And another says, "This is the assurance we have in Him." So it takes the words, "confidence," "boldness," and "assurance" to mean what God meant when He said, "This is that which we feel toward Him."

Right here comes the parting of the ways between the man of faith and the man of unfaith. The man of unfaith rejects flatly this kind of teaching: that this is the confidence that we have in Him, that if we ask anything according to His will, He will give it to us. The man of unfaith says that this can't be so. And he will not accept it and he demands the proof of human reason.

Unbelief is not a mental thing at all, but a moral thing. Unbelief is always sinful because it almost presupposes an immoral condition of the heart before it can exist. Unbelief is not the failure of the mind to grasp the truth; it is not a bad conclusion drawn from logical premises; and it is not the failure of unsoundness of a logical premise. It is a moral sin. But we'll leave that aside for a little bit and simply say that the man of unfaith cannot understand the language that I'm giving you now. This is the confidence that we have in God – that if we ask anything according to His will, He heareth us. Jesus said, "If you ask anything in my name I will do it."

The man without faith says, "I've got to have a reason for this." The man of faith feels confidence. The man of faith does not dare rest upon human reasoning.

I have wondered sometimes why somebody didn't come out; and say that I have used reason to prove that reason was no good. But, here is what I have done: I have used reason to do what reason CAN do – mainly to show that there are some things that reason cannot do. I have never been against human reason, but I have been against human reason trying to do things human reason is not qualified to do.

The great difference today in the world is not between the liberal and the fundamentalist. But the great gulf fixed today is between the evangelical rationalist and the evangelical mystic, the one who believes God and disbelieves human reason and the one who believes the things of God can be proved by and grasped by human reason.

I won't live to see it, but some of you younger people will live to see that I am right in what I am saying. We have evangelical rationalists who insist upon trying to reduce everything down to where it can be explained and proved. The result is that we have rationalized faith and we have pulled Almighty God down to the low level of human reason. There are some things human reason cannot do. But you can use human reason to discredit human reason. Anything human reason can do, I'm for it. Turn human reason loose. You have a can opener in your house. And what woman doesn't? You don't use it to mend your little boy's stocking. You use it to open cans. Your husband has a hammer and a saw; he doesn't use them to paper the walls of the living room. He uses them to cut boards and pounds nails. Everything was created for a purpose, and I claim that there are some things human reason cannot do.

Human reason and faith are not contrary to each other, but one is above the other. When we are believers, we enter another world altogether, a realm that is infinite above little reason. "My thoughts are not your thoughts, nor are my ways your ways." As high as the heaven is above the earth so are the thoughts of God above the thoughts of man. Faith never goes contrary to reason; faith simply ignores reason and rises above it.

Reason could not tell us that Jesus Christ should be born of the Virgin Mary, but faith knows He was. Reason cannot prove that Jesus took upon Him the form of a man and died under the sins of the world, but faith knows that He did. Reason cannot prove that the third day He rose from the dead, but faith knows that He did. Faith is an organ of knowledge.

Fundamental rationalists say the human brain alone is an organ of knowledge. They forget there are at lest two other organs of knowledge. Feeling is an organ of knowledge, too. All the reasoning in the world couldn't tell you the temperature was 98 today. You felt that is was. I can stand heat like a lizard, but I've had enough of this. And I know it was hot today. I had an organ of knowledge today—feeling.

A young man loves a young woman. How does he know it? Does he read the Encyclopedia Britannia and apply reason to it? No. He listens to the ticking of his own heart. He knows it by feeling. Feeling is an organ of knowledge. Reason is an organ of knowledge and faith is an organ of knowledge. And we have to believe that.

Reason cannot say, "Jesus rose from the dead." Faith knows He did. Reason cannot say, "He sits at the right hand of God Father Almighty." Reason doesn't know, but faith knows that He did. Reason cannot say, "He shall come to judge the quick and the dead." But faith knows that He will come. Reason cannot say, "My sins are all gone." But faith knows they're gone. So, all down the line, faith is an organ of knowledge. And the man who believes is having knowledge that the man who merely thinks can't possibly have. Our poor little old brain can come staggering along like a little boy trying to keep up with his dad—coming along on his little, old, short, stubby legs, trying to reason.

That's why in the New Testament the word "wonder" appears. "And they wondered at him." "And they all marveled." Faith was going ahead, doing wonders, and reason was coming along, wide-eyed, marveling. That's always the way it should be.

Nowadays, we send reason ahead on his little, short legs, and faith never follows. Nobody marvels because they can explain the whole business. I claim that a Christian is a miracle and just the moment you can explain a Christian, you have no Christian left anymore.

Some of you may have read William James' *Varieties of Religious Experiences*. I've read it two or three times.

It's helpful to me because I'm a man of faith. But William James tried to understand the wonders of God working in the human breast through psychology. But when the early disciples were on Solomon's porch in prayer and praise, people stood back awe-struck and dared not join themselves to them. And the real Christian is somebody that can't be explained by human reason. Something happens that psychology cannot explain. Faith is the highest kind of reason. Faith takes us straight into the Presence of God and goes behind the veil where also our Lord Jesus Christ, our Forerunner has gone for us, and engages God Almighty and reaches that for which He was created. It is here where the man of faith communes with the source of his being and loves the Fountain of his life and prays to the One who begot him, and knows the God who made Heaven and Earth. He may not be an astronomer, but he knows the God who made the stars. He may not be a physicist, but he knows the God who made mathematics.

# PureGoldClassics
## TimelessTruthinaDistinctiveBest-SellingCollection

An Expanding Collection of the Best-Loved Christian Classics of All Time.
## AVAILABLE AT FINE BOOKSTORES.
FOR MORE INFORMATION, VISIT WWW.BRIDGELOGOS.COM

THE HOLY SPIRIT POWER — Includes 10 Timeless Messages — Classic — JOHN WESLEY

THE HOLY CATHOLIC CHURCH — Classic — JOHN CALVIN

HUMILITY — Classic — ANDREW MURRAY

THE IMITATION OF CHRIST — After the Bible, this is probably the best-loved book of Christendom — Classic — THOMAS à KEMPIS

IN HIS STEPS — Millions of copies sold in over 41 countries — Classic — CHARLES M. SHELDON

INTERIOR CASTLE — The Soul's Spiritual Journey in Union with God — Classic — TERESA OF AVILA

JEWELS FROM E. M. BOUNDS — Classic — E.M. BOUNDS

THE KNEELING CHRISTIAN — Includes The Life of Prayer by A. B. Simpson and The True Vine, H. Meditation by Andrew Murray — Classic — AN UNKNOWN CHRISTIAN

MADAME JEANNE GUYON — EXPERIENCING UNION WITH GOD THROUGH INNER PRAYER & THE WAY AND RESULTS OF UNION WITH GOD

MORNING BY MORNING — Classic — CHARLES H. SPURGEON

OBTAINING THE GRACE OF CHRIST — Classic — Book 3 from the Magnum Opus of Christian Theology INSTITUTES OF THE CHRISTIAN RELIGION — JOHN CALVIN

THE OVERCOMING LIFE — Classic — D. L. MOODY

THE PILGRIM'S PROGRESS IN MODERN ENGLISH — Classic — JOHN BUNYAN

POWER, PASSION & PRAYER — Finney's Greatest Sermons on Revival through Prayer — Classic — CHARLES G. FINNEY

THE PRACTICE OF THE PRESENCE OF GOD — Classic — BROTHER LAWRENCE

SECRET POWER — Classic — D.L. MOODY

A SERIOUS CALL TO A DEVOUT & HOLY LIFE — Classic — WILLIAM LAW

THE SERMON ON THE MOUNT — Classic — JOHN WESLEY

SINNERS IN THE HANDS OF AN ANGRY GOD — Classic — JONATHAN EDWARDS

THE SOVEREIGNTY OF GOD — Classic — A.W. PINK

SPURGEON ON THE BLOOD OF CHRIST — Classic — CHARLES H. SPURGEON

SPURGEON ON CHRIST — Classic — CHARLES H. SPURGEON

SPURGEON ON GOD — Classic — CHARLES H. SPURGEON

SPURGEON ON THE HOLY SPIRIT — Classic — CHARLES H. SPURGEON

SPURGEON ON PRAYER — Classic — CHARLES H. SPURGEON

SPURGEON ON THE PSALMS — BOOK ONE — Psalm 1 through Psalm 25 — Classic — CHARLES H. SPURGEON

SPURGEON ON THE PSALMS — BOOK TWO — Psalm 26 through Psalm 50 — Classic — CHARLES H. SPURGEON

SPURGEON ON THE PSALMS — BOOK THREE — Psalm 51 through Psalm 79 — Classic — CHARLES H. SPURGEON

TABLE TALK — MARTIN LUTHER — Classic

TORREY ON PRAYER — Classic — THE POWER OF PRAYER & THE PRAYER OF POWER

TOZER — Classic — FELLOWSHIP OF THE BURNING HEART

TOZER: MYSTERY OF THE HOLY SPIRIT — Classic — A.W. TOZER

WALKING WITH GOD — Classic — THE ANDREW MURRAY TRILOGY ON SANCTIFICATION

WILLIAM WILBERFORCE — Classic — GREATEST WORKS

WITH CHRIST IN THE SCHOOL OF PRAYER — Classic — ANDREW MURRAY